Team Up! 4

ACTIVITY BOOK

Suzanne Roy
Kathleen Vatcher

5757, Rue Cypihot, Montréal (Québec) H4S 1R3
Téléphone : (514) 334-2690 • Télécopieur : (514) 334-4720
erpidlm@odyssee.net

ENGLISH AS A SECOND LANGUAGE – GRADE 4

Project editor: **Jeanine Floyd**

Book design and page layout: **Miller Graphistes Conseils Inc.**

Cover design: **Dumont Gratton**

Illustrations:
Christine Battuz, Josée Dombrowski, Daniel Dumont, Jean-Paul Eid, Lucie Faniel, Marie-Claude Favreau, Claire Lemieux, Caroline Merola

Dépôt légal : 1er trimestre 1998
Bibliothèque nationale du Québec
Bibliothèque nationale du Canada
Imprimé au Canada

ISBN 2-7613-0651-1

1234567890 IE 987
30008 ABCD OF2-10

Contents

Note to the teacher

This Activity Book has been designed to be used with the *Team Up! 4* Student's Book. It replaces most of the teaching handouts and all the Check-up time handouts provided in the Teacher's Guide. (See following list.) It therefore saves you the time and effort you would otherwise spend making photocopies.

To make it easier for the students, we have used pictograms rather than instructions. These are described on page vi. Before you start working with this Activity Book, take a few moments to go over the pictograms with the students and make sure they understand them.

For teachers who wish to give their students independent work to do in class or as homework, an extra activity is supplied at the end of each unit.

The following handouts are **not** covered in this book:
3, 7T, 10T, 20T, 22T, 24T, 25T, 35 36T, 37T, 38T, 39T, 44a+b, 45, 46, 48T, 49T.

Chers parents,

Ce programme a pour objectif d'aider votre enfant à utiliser l'anglais dans sa vie de tous les jours. Le materiel Team Up ! vise à amener les élèves à se servir de l'anglais pour communiquer. Pour atteindre cet objectif, les élèves doivent acquérir quatre habiletés langagières – la compréhension orale, la compréhension écrite, l'expression orale et l'expression écrite – en utilisant différents types de textes sur des sujets variés. Tout au long de l'année, ils seront appelés à comprendre et à rédiger des textes simples en anglais.

Vous pouvez aider votre enfant à améliorer sa compétence en anglais en lui lisant des histoires, en l'incitant à lire des livres ou des magazines en anglais, en l'encourageant à s'exercer à parler anglais lorsque la situation s'y prête, ainsi qu'en lui donnant l'occasion de se " faire l'oreille " au moyen d'émissions télévisées ou de musique de langue anglaise. Tous ces moyens sont bons pour aider votre enfant à développer les habiletés requises en anglais.

Au cours de l'année, votre enfant travaillera en groupes d'apprentissage coopératif, c'est-à-dire qu'il ou elle travaillera avec ses camarades au sein de petites équipes. Les équipes seront appelées à accomplir diverses tâches et chaque élève, au sein de son équipe, devra en assumer une partie. Pour que les équipes puissent mener à bien les tâches qui leur sont assignées, il faut donc que chaque élève fasse sa part. Dans le cadre de ce materiel, les enfants sont encouragés à être responsables de leur apprentissage et à participer activement à leur cheminement scolaire.

Vous pourrez communiquer avec moi tout au long de l'année scolaire. Si vous avez des questions concernant les objectifs du cours ou le programme d'apprentissage coopératif, n'hésitez pas à me les poser.

Dans l'attente de vous rencontrer,
recevez mes salutations amicales

Key

Picto	Means	Example
	Write.	ACTIVITY 1 **What do you know?** SB 140
	Draw or colour.	My favourite month
✓	**Put a checkmark next to your answer.**	**Reflection** **Did you . . .** . . . listen to your teammates? ❑ ❑ . . . share your ideas and opinions? ❑ ❑ (Yes ✓ / No ✓)
Match! Match! Match!	**Find the matching parts.**	Match! Match! Match! January, February, March, April, May, June July, August, September, October, November, December

UNIT 1

All about us

ACTIVITY 1 Meeting people

Meet my friend ______________________.

Pleased to ______________ ______________.

ACTIVITY 2 Hooray for the class!

Hi! My name is ______________________.

My birthday is on ______________________.

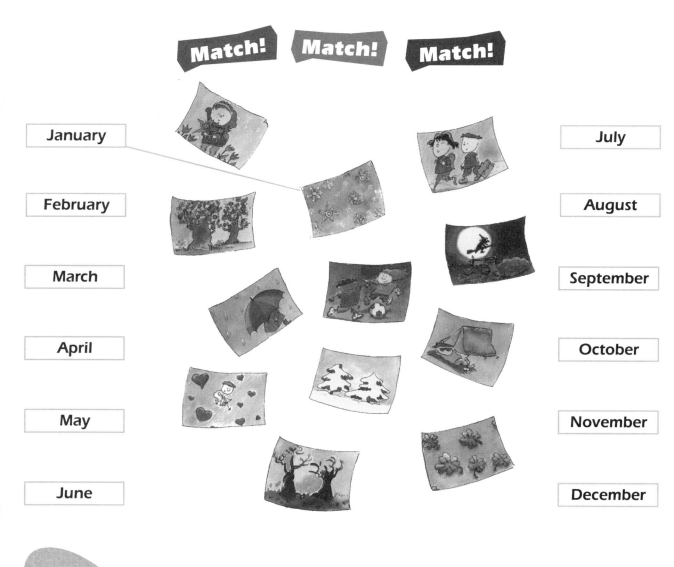

Match! Match! Match!

January		July
February		August
March		September
April		October
May		November
June		December

ACTIVITY 3 Same or different?

My favourite pastimes	Same ✓	Different ✓
▶ Sports ______	◯	◯
▶ Collecting ______	◯	◯
▶ Games ______	◯	◯
▶ Other activities ______	◯	◯

ACTIVITY 4 Fact or fiction?

Name ______________________

Date of birth ______________________

Address ______________________

____

Telephone number ______________________

Age ____________ Grade ____________

Hair colour ______________________

Eye colour ______________________

Height ______________________

ACTIVITY 5 Who are we?

SB 7

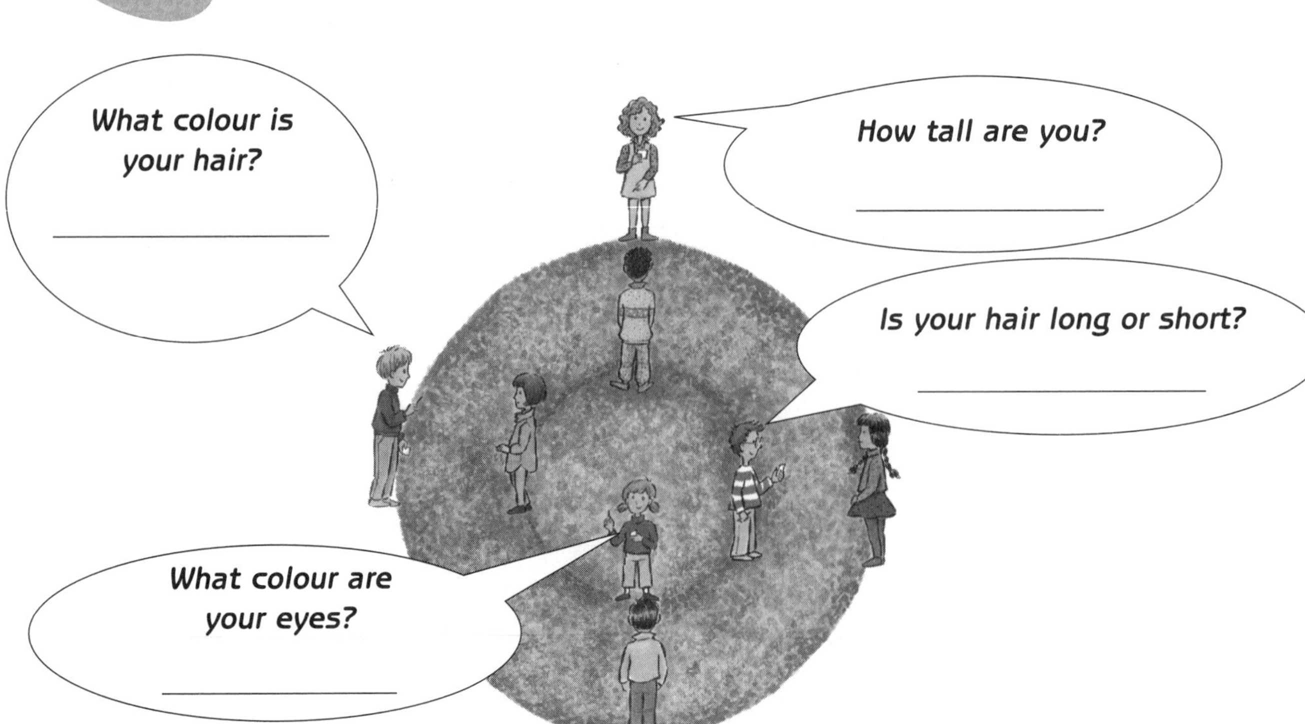

What colour is your hair?
How tall are you?
Is your hair long or short?
What colour are your eyes?

Who's who?

All about me

Me

1 Hi! I'm ____________________.

2 I like ____________________.

3

My pet

My favourite family member

____

____

____

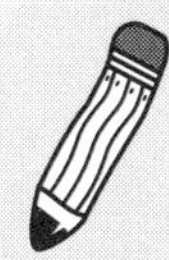

Name: Sean Kavanagh
Date of birth: September 14, 1989
Address: 264 Campbell Street, Montréal
Telephone number: 362-2867
Age: 9
Grade: 4
Hair colour: Black
Eye colour: Green
Height: 120 cm

NAME:
Sean Kavanagh

FAVOURITE PASTIMES:
Reading and playing video games

FAVOURITE SPORT:
Hockey

FAVOURITE MUSIC:
Rock

Fill in the missing information.

This is ______________________________.

He is __________ years old. He is in grade __________.

Sean lives in ______________________. He has ______________ eyes and ____________________ hair. He is __________ tall.

Sean's favourite sport is ______________________. He likes to listen to ______________________. He also likes to ______________________ and to play ______________________ in his spare time.

Check-up TIME

SB 9

This is what I learned.

	Yes ✓	No ✓
1 I can . . .		
. . . greet someone.	❑	❑
. . . introduce my friend.	❑	❑
2 I can . . .		
. . . give my name.	❑	❑
. . . give my address	❑	❑
. . . give my birthday.	❑	❑
. . . give my telephone number.	❑	❑
. . . say what I like to do.	❑	❑
. . . say what grade I'm in.	❑	❑
. . . give my age.	❑	❑
3 I can . . .		
. . . say what colour my eyes are.	❑	❑
. . . say if I'm short or tall.	❑	❑
. . . say what colour my hair is.	❑	❑

Reflection

Did you . . .		
. . . work well?	❑	❑
. . . move quietly?	❑	❑

UNIT 2

Absent-minded Alex

ACTIVITY 1

Are you forgetful?

1

2

Yes ✓ ❑ No ✓ ❑

3

Yes ✓ ❑ No ✓ ❑

4

6

5

7

The story, part one

Who?	Absent-minded Alex	What?
____________		____________

Where?

____

Match! Match! Match!

1. Who is happy?
2. Where is my book?
3. What is it?
4. Who is it ?
5. Where is Alex?

at home
Alex
Mr Wylie
a ruler
on the desk

ACTIVITY 3

Where are my things?

The story, part 2

ACTIVITY 5

The story, the conclusion

Alex feels ______________________________.

Alex feels ______________________________.

Alex feels ______________________________.

I think the story is ______________________.

The complete story

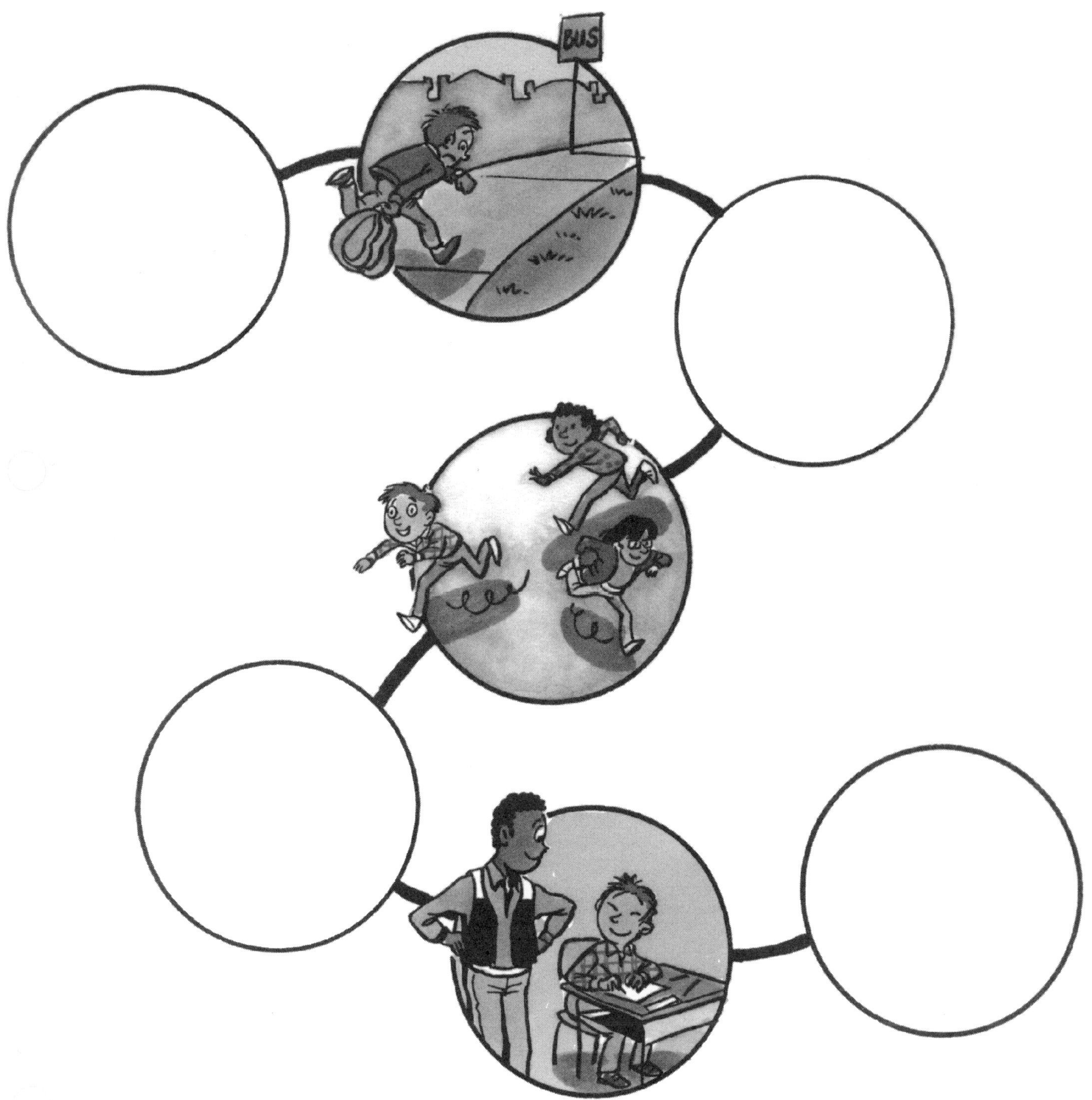

Absent-minded Liz?

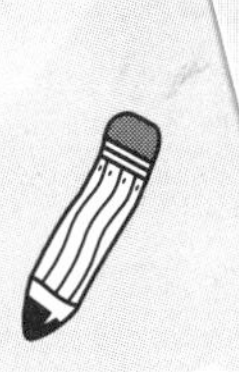

How many things can you name?

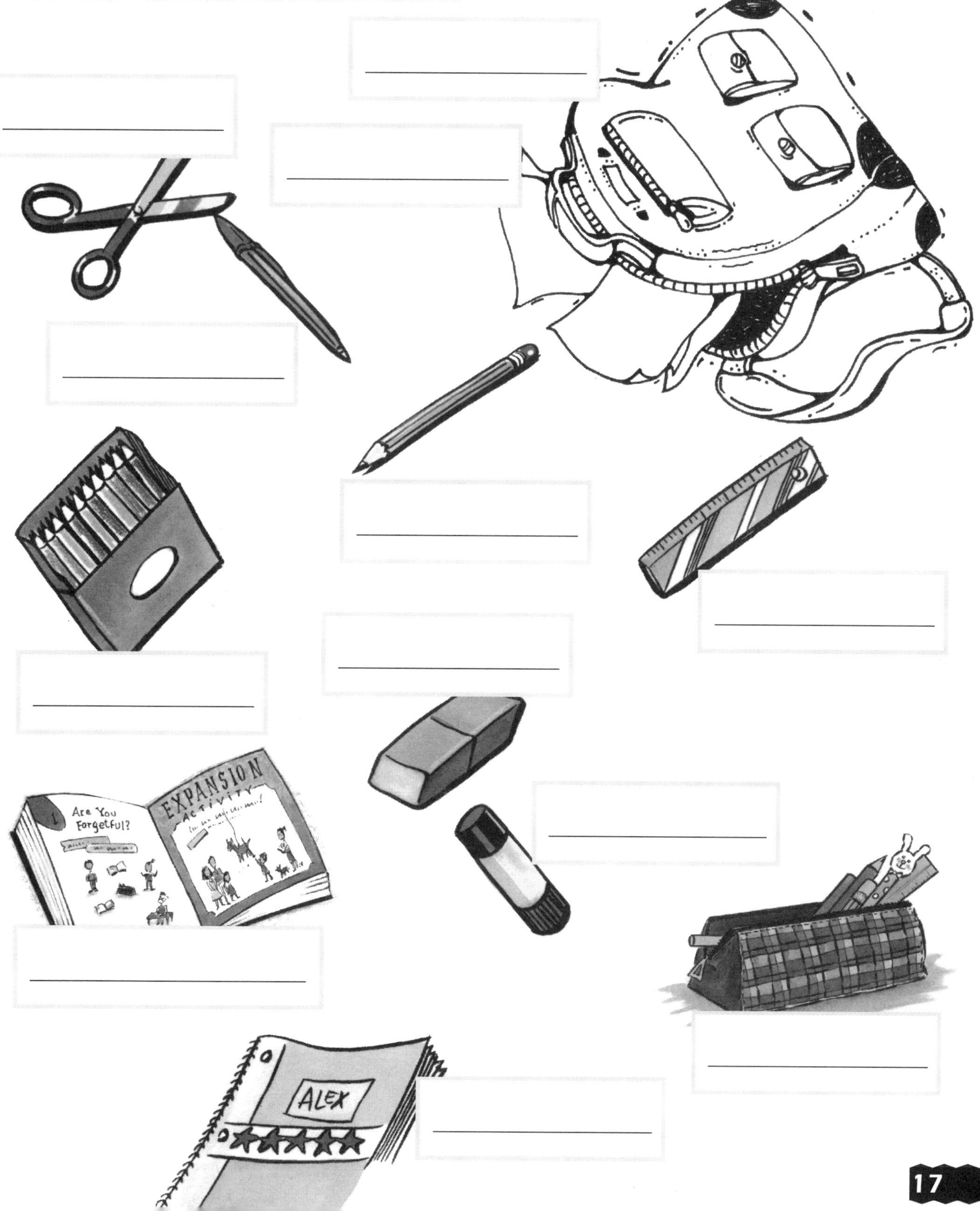

Check-up TIME

SB 21

This is what I learned.

	Yes ✓	No ✓
1 **I can name my school supplies.**	❑	❑
2 **I can name the characters from the story.**	❑	❑
3 **I can answer these questions.**		
▪ Who is forgetful?	❑	❑
▪ What did Alex forget?	❑	❑
▪ Where did Alex forget his schoolbag?	❑	❑
4 **I can give my reactions to the story.**	❑	❑

I think "**Absent-minded Alex**" was ______________________________ .

Reflection

Did you . . .

. . . move quietly in your group?	❑	❑
. . . take turns?	❑	❑
. . . work quietly?	❑	❑

UNIT 3

Happy Birthday!

ACTIVITY 1 Birthday celebrations

1. We eat __ __ __ __ and candies at parties.
2. Funny people: __ __ __ __ __ __ .
3. Origin of birthday parties: __ __ __ __ __ __ __ .
4. Two __ __ __ __ __ __ __ __ sisters composed a birthday song.
5. An old birthday celebration was called __ __ __ __ __ __ __ __ __ __ .

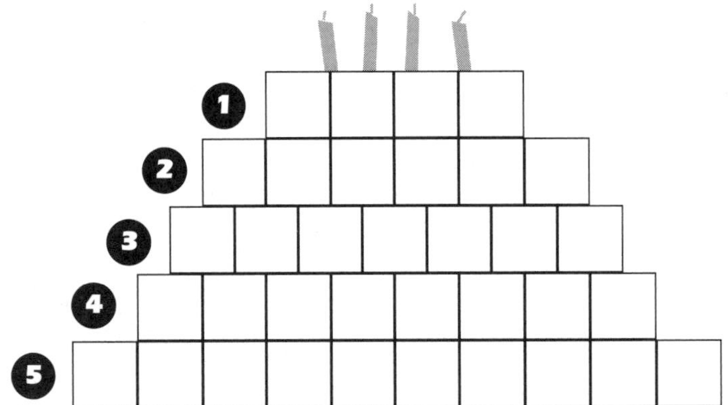

ACTIVITY 2 Birthdays around the world

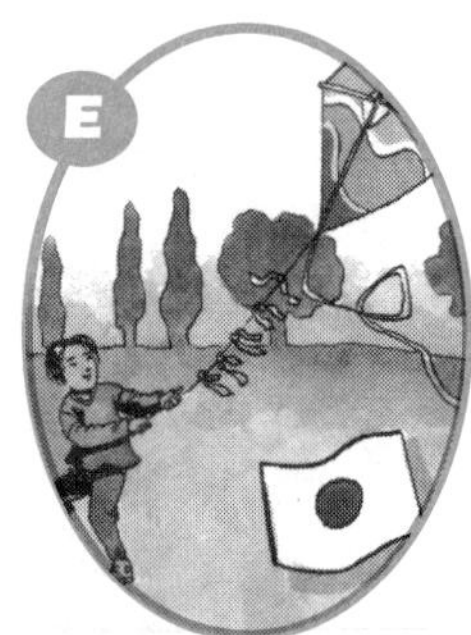

Birthday calendar

January	February	March
April	May	June
July	August	September
October	November	December

ACTIVITY 4

Let's have a suggestion box

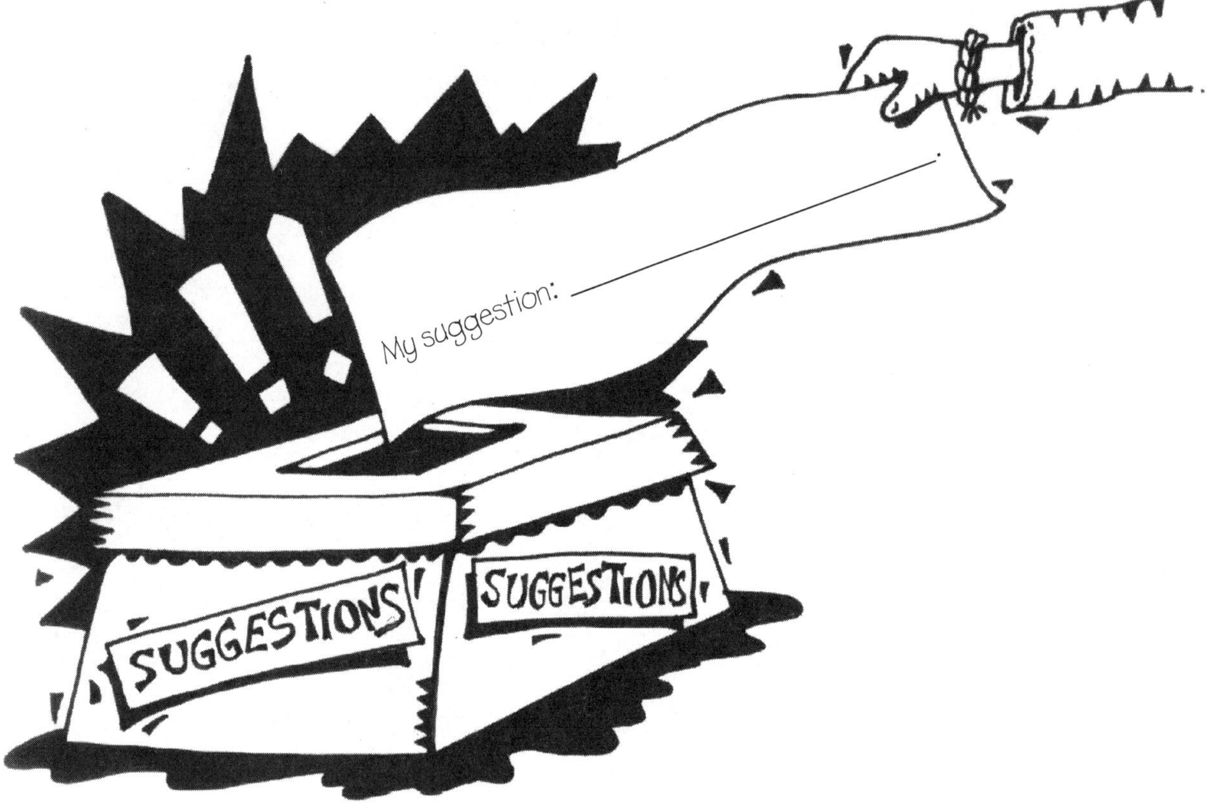

ACTIVITY 5

Planning something special

My team ________________________________

____

What we're making ____________________________

My job __________________________________

Happy Birthday!

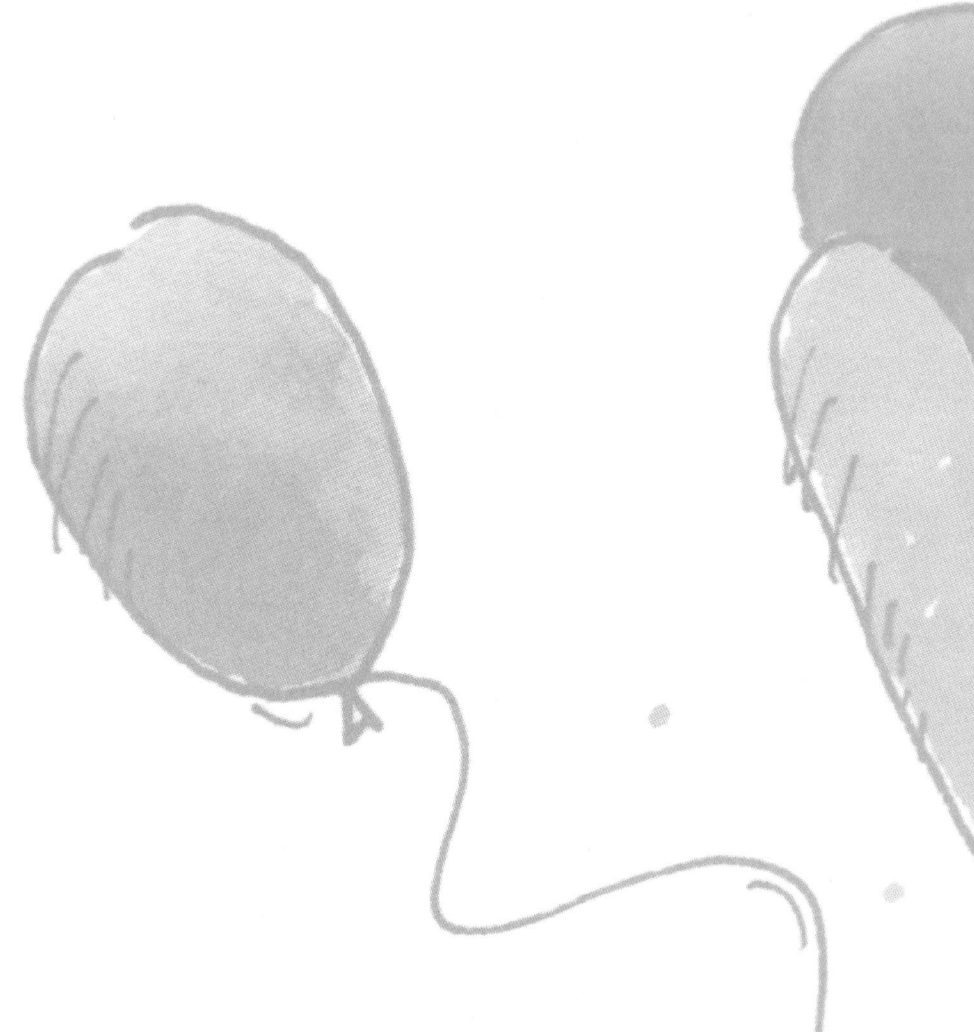

My birthday message

____

The pineta

In Mexico, family and friends are invited to celebrate birthdays and special occasions by breaking a pineta. A pineta is a pot made of dried mud in the form of an animal. It is painted and decorated with bright coloured paper. It is filled with surprises such as candy and party favours. Someone hangs the pineta in the middle of the yard on a long string. The birthday person is blindfolded and given a stick. The guests watch him or her hit the pineta until it breaks open and all the surprises fall to the ground. The guests hurry to pick up the surprises.

Write the instruction words.

Colour the balloons.

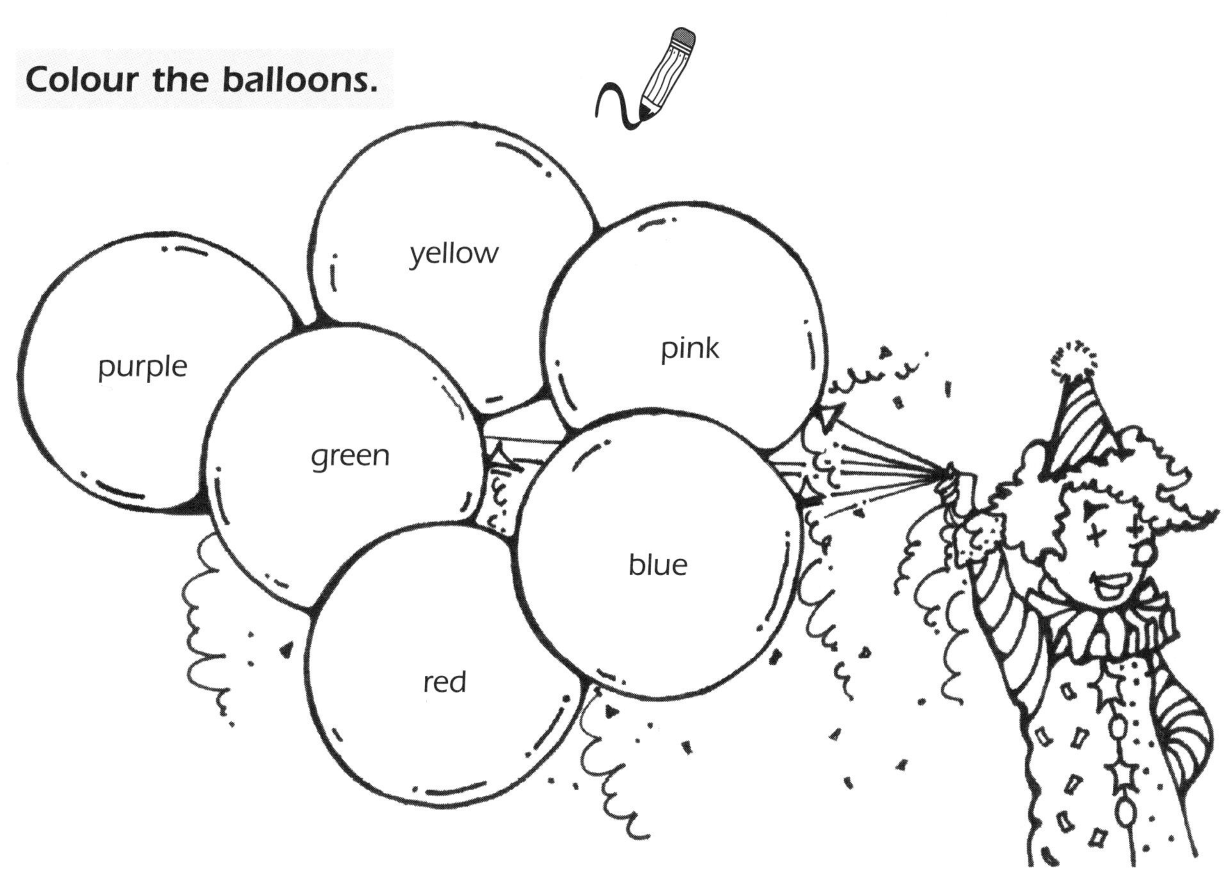

Check-up TIME

SB 31

This is what I learned.

	Yes ✓	No ✓
1 **I can say . . .**		
. . . **who** wrote the Happy Birthday song.	❑	❑
. . . **where** birthday parties began.	❑	❑
. . . **how** the Japanese people celebrate birthdays.	❑	❑
. . . **how** children in the Netherlands celebrate birthdays.	❑	❑
. . . **how** I celebrate my birthday.	❑	❑
2 **I can . . .**		
. . . suggest ideas.	❑	❑
. . . follow instructions.	❑	❑

Reflection

Did you . . .

. . .work well in your group?	❑	❑
. . . listen to your teammates' ideas?	❑	❑
. . . share ideas?	❑	❑

UNIT 4

Different Families

ACTIVITY 1 Meet Amélie's family

ACTIVITY 2 Reuben's family

ACTIVITY 3 Lee's family

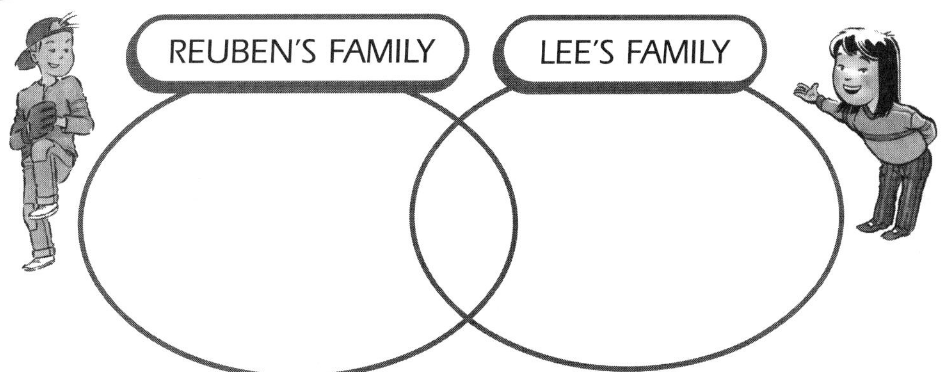

ACTIVITY 4 Jason's family

On weekdays

On weekends

ACTIVITY 5

My family

CLOSURE

My special object: ______________________________

It belongs to: ______________________________

EXPANSION ACTIVITY

SB 42

Tighten your family bonds

Some more ideas

____

____

____

Write everyone's title.
Don't forget the extended family!

Check-up TIME

SB 41

This is what I learned.

1 **How many people are there in your family?** ☐

Can you name them? Yes ✓ ☐ No ✓ ☐

2 **How many people are there in your partner's family?** ☐

Can you name them? Yes ✓ ☐ No ✓ ☐

3 **Can you compare your family with your partner's family?** Yes ✓ ☐ No ✓ ☐

Reflection

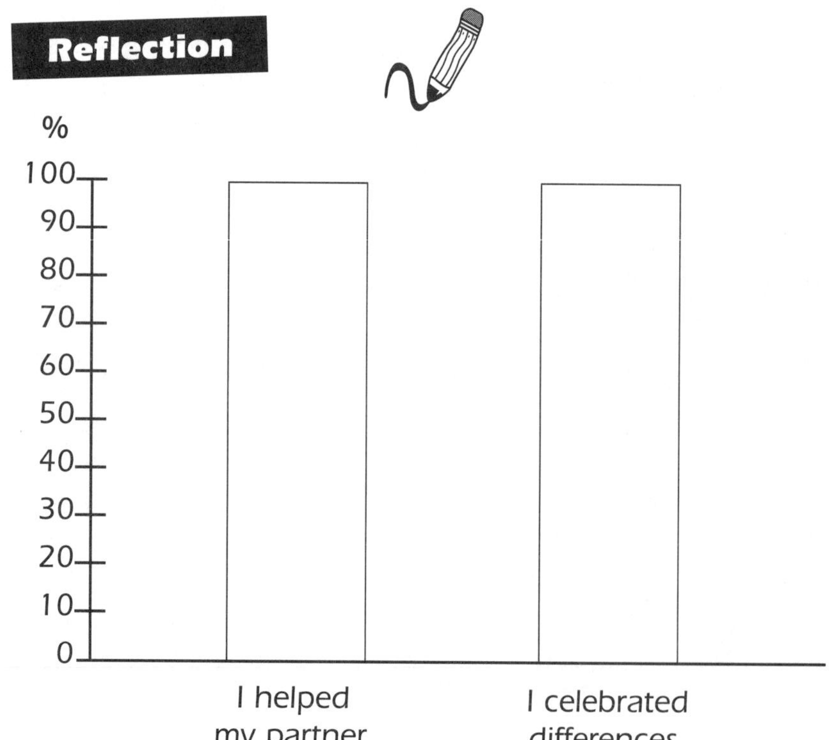

UNIT 5

Tender, Loving Care

A second chance

CHARACTERS	OBJECTS	ANIMALS
Matthew	rug	fish

ACTIVITY 2

Animal talk

What the pet wants	What the pet owner should do	My answer was: Correct ✓	My answer was: Incorrect ✓
1	**Feed it.**	❑	❑
2	**Pet it.**	❑	❑
3	**Play with it.**	❑	❑
4	**Give it water.**	❑	❑
5	**Take it for a walk.**	❑	❑
6	**Change the litter.**	❑	❑

ACTIVITY 3 A quiet moment

Matthew likes his pets. ✔ ❑

Matthew doesn't like his pets. ✔ ❑

I like my pet. ✔ ❑

I don't like my pet. ✔ ❑

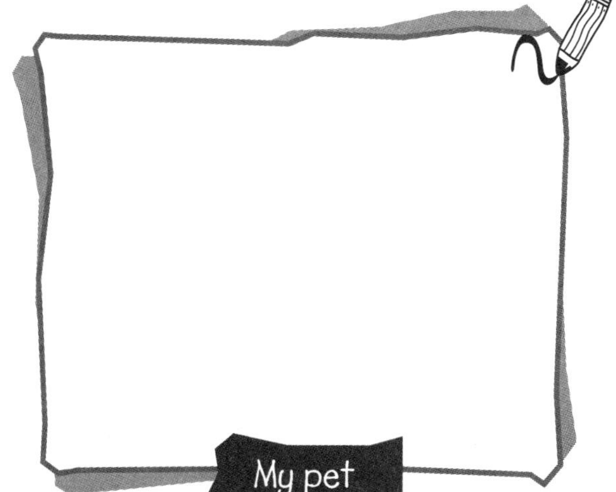

ACTIVITY 4 Pet care

My pet is a ______________________.

HOUSE

____

FOOD/DRINK

____

CARE

____

ATTENTION

Love your pet and talk to it!

ACTIVITY 5

The promise

Characters

Problems

Resolution

ANIMAL KINDNESS WEEK

Animal read-a-thon!

Title of story ____________________

Characters

____

____

____

Problems

____

____

____

Resolution

____

____

____

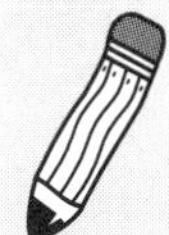

- Look at the picture for two minutes.
- Close your book.
- Write down all the things you can remember or tell your partner.

Check-up TIME

SB 53

This is what I learned.

	Yes ✓	No ✓
1 I can name the characters in the story.	❑	❑
2 I know what to do with my dog.	❑	❑

3 My favourite pet is a ______________________________

I don't like ______________________________

Reflection

Did you . . .

	Yes ✓	No ✓
. . . encourage others?	❑	❑
. . . participate in your team?	❑	❑
. . . feel good about your work?	❑	❑

UNIT 6

Magic Time!

ACTIVITY 1 What do you know?

ACTIVITY 2 Make a magic wand

Fill in the gaps.

1 Make sure you have tape, ____________, aluminum paper, black construction paper and a pencil.

2 Take the ____________ and place it so that one corner faces you.

3 ____________ the black paper round the ____________ .

4 Tape the ____________ and remove the pencil.

5 ____________ both ends inside the ____________ .

6 ____________ a piece of aluminum paper 60 X 40 mm and cut it.

7 Roll the ____________ paper round one end of the tube and tape it.

ACTIVITY 3 I can do that!

	Magic tricks	Can ✓	Can't ✓	Need(s) help ✓
1	Making balls float in the air			
2	Making a coin disappear			
3	Doing card tricks			

ACTIVITY 4 Let the show begin!

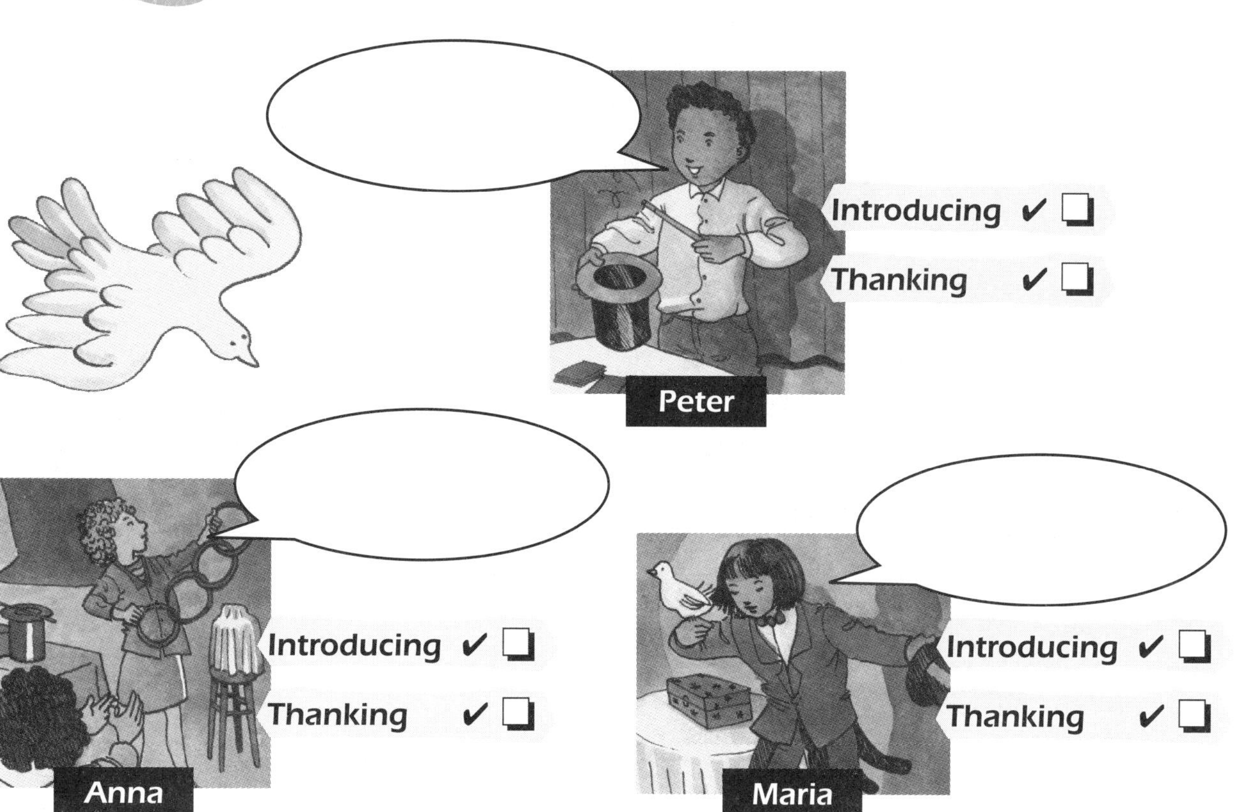

CLOSURE

My trick: ______________________________

Materials: ______________________________

____

Introducing myself: Hi, I'm ______________________________

Thanking the audience: ______________________________

Spot the six differences!

Check-up TIME

SB 60

This is what I learned.

		Yes ✓	No ✓
1	**I can introduce myself and my friend.**	❑	❑
	I can thank someone.	❑	❑
	I can follow simple instructions.	❑	❑

Reflection

Did you . . .

	Yes ✓	No ✓
. . . encourage your partner?	❑	❑
. . . help your partner?	❑	❑

Winter Fun!

ACTIVITY 1

Brrr! It's winter.

ACTIVITY 2

Yes, I can!

ACTIVITY 3

Where do these sports come from?

Skiing

1. What did people use to travel over the snow?

2. Where was skiing invented?

3. When did people start skiing for fun?

Snowmobiling

1. Who invented the snowmobile?

____

2. What year was the snowmobile invented?

____

3. Where was the snowmobile invented?

____

Ice hockey

1. Where did ice hockey begin?

____

2. What similar sport is played on grass?

____

3. What is the oldest sport in the world?

____

ACTIVITY 4 Backyard fun

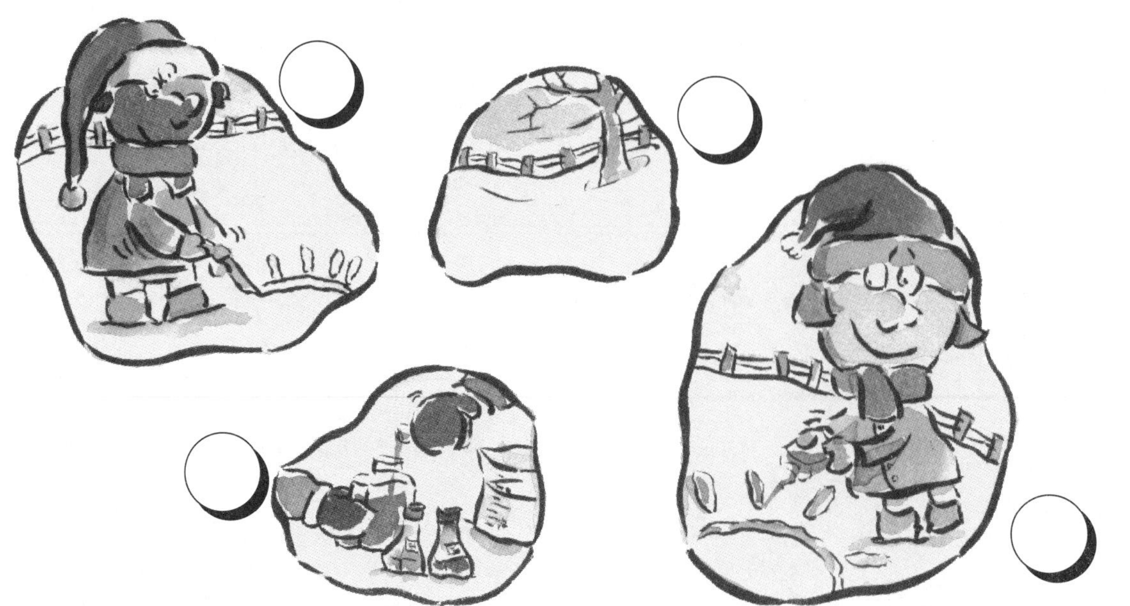

Group	1	2	3	4	5	6	7
Winter scene							
Winter activities							
Originality							
Colours							
Slogan							
TOTAL							

Points **3** = Excellent **2** = Good **1** = Fair

Snow

What's in the trunk?

What are they doing?

Check-up TIME

This is what I learned.

1 **Can you do these activities?**

2 **Can you answer these questions?**

Where did ice hockey start?

____

Who invented the snowmobile?

____

What sport was invented in Sweden?

____

3 **Can you understand the instructions? Draw your answer.**

1. Make a large snowball.
2. Make a medium snowball. Put it on the large ball.
3. Make another small snowball. Put it on the medium ball. That's the head.
4. Use stones to make eyes and a nose.
5. Use red food colouring to make a mouth.
6. Paint blue buttons on the body.
7. Put a hat on the head and a warm scarf around the neck.

What have you got?

Reflection

Did you. . .

	Yes ✓	No ✓
. . . participate?	❑	❑
. . . listen to others?	❑	❑
. . . let others give their ideas?	❑	❑

UNIT 8

Jenny Lives on Hunter Street

Where are you?

Questions

Questions

Questions

Questions

Questions

Questions

Questions

Questions

Jenny lives on Hunter Street

Before listening

1. Write down the title of the story.

2. Look at the illustrations on SB pages 74-77. Look for clues about the story. Write them down.

People (Who?)

Places (Where?)

Events (What happened?)

3 Circle the words that you know.

think · Saturday · house · walk · right-hand · live · across · play · street · come

While listening

4 Listen for the words and expressions that you know.

Circle the clues in #2 that were right.

After listening

5 What is the story about? Write down any extra information.

ACTIVITY 3 Jenny and me

Jenny	Me
▪ Hunter Street ▪ Number 48 ▪ across the park	▪ ______ ▪ ______ ▪ ______

ACTIVITY 4 That's where Jenny lives.

ACTIVITY 5 Can you find me?

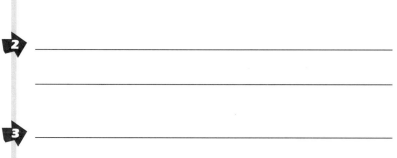

To get from ______________________________ to ______________________________

DIRECTIONS

1 ______________________________

____

2 ______________________________

____

3 ______________________________

____

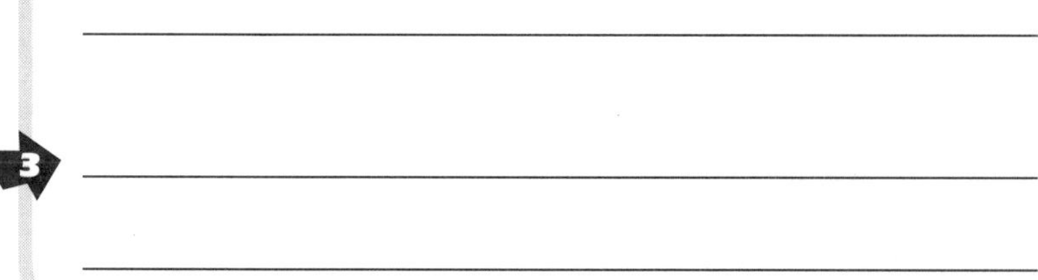

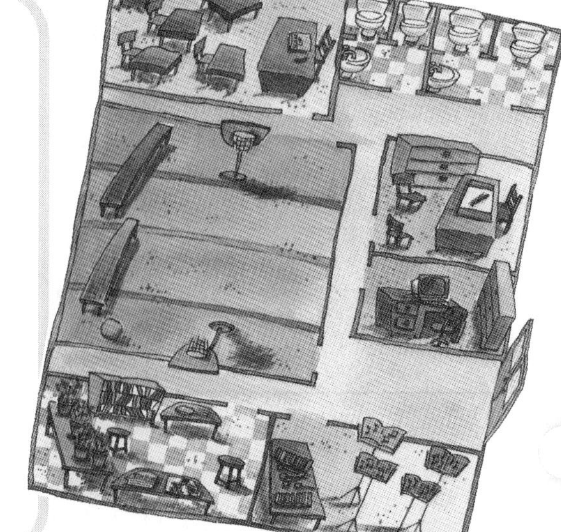

SB 80

______ Lives on ______ Street

1

______ can't come to my house.

______ can't come to play.

______ can't come to my house.

______ doesn't know the way.

2

______ lives on ______ Street.

And I live ______ .

It isn't far to ______ Street.

I think I know the way.

3

We need to walk down ______ Street,

Along the ______ side,

And here we are on ______ Street.

The number's ______ .

4

Now ______ can come to my house.

Maybe next Saturday?

______ can come to my house.

The map shows ______ the way.

To get from ____________
to ____________

DIRECTIONS

1 ______________________________

____

____

____

2 ______________________________

____

____

____

3 ______________________________

____

____

____

PINE STREET
POST OFFICE
LIBRARY
STREET
KING STREET
STREET
HOSPITAL
SCHOOL
HOLLAND STREET

Draw a town. Include the things and buildings in the list.

Label the places.

house

school

bank

post office

library

hospital

police station

fire station

gate

bridge

Check-up TIME

SB 81

This is what I learned.

1 **I can name lots of places.**

	BANK		POLICE STATION	FIRE STATION	Shopping Centre	
Yes ✓	❑	❑	❑	❑	❑	❑
No ✓	❑	❑	❑	❑	❑	❑

	Yes ✓	No ✓
2 **Do you eat in a library?**	❑	❑
Do you sleep in a restaurant?	❑	❑
Do you go shopping at a police station?	❑	❑
3 **Do you know the way to the fire station?**	❑	❑

Reflection

Did you . . .

. . . take turns in your team?	❑	❑
. . . listen to others talk?	❑	❑
. . . help your partners?	❑	❑

Are you . . .

. . . happy about your team's work?	❑	❑

UNIT 9

The Inventor

Check it out!

Can you find these things at home?

skate

Yes ✔ ❑ No ✔ ❑

basketball and net

Yes ✔ ❑ No ✔ ❑

dial telephone

Yes ✔ ❑ No ✔ ❑

paint roller

Yes ✔ ❑ No ✔ ❑

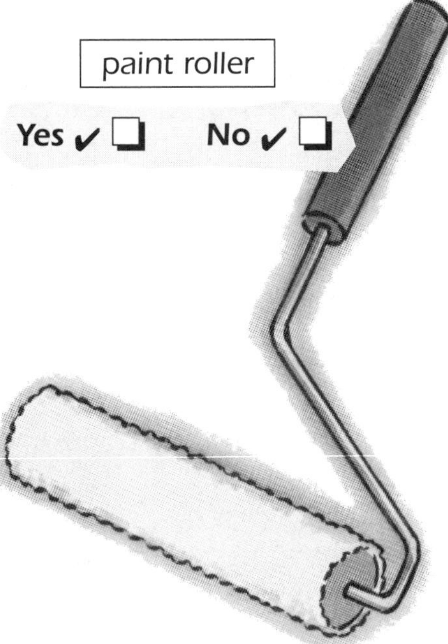

light bulb

Yes ✔ ❑ No ✔ ❑

snowmobile

Yes ✔ ❑ No ✔ ❑

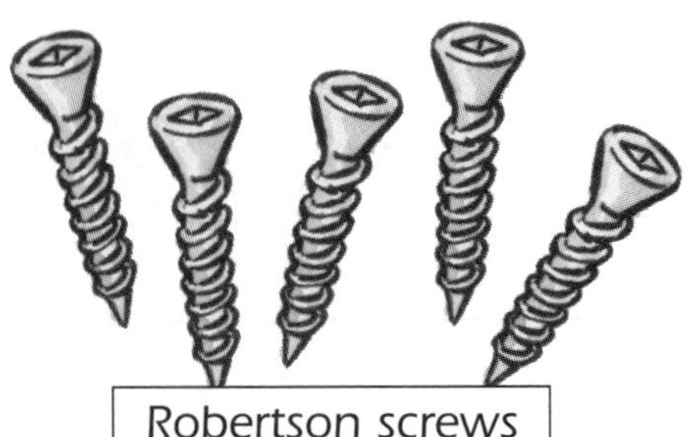

Robertson screws

Yes ✔ ❑ No ✔ ❑

Mothers of invention

Match!

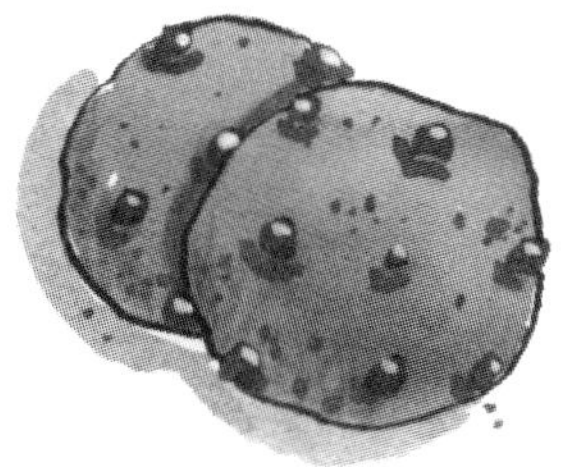

ACTIVITY 3

Unusual uses

ACTIVITY 4

Invention Whiz Quiz

1.	T			V		S					
2.			L		P	H					
3.	T		B			■			C		Y
4.	S	K									
5.	B			K			B				

My own invention

Invention name game

1. Name an invention that begins with the letter **C**.

   ____

2. Name an invention that is good to eat.

   ____

3. Name an invention you have in your bedroom.

   ____

4. Name an invention you can find in space.

   ____

5. Name an invention that makes a noise.

   ____

6. Name an invention you use at school.

   ____

7. Name an old invention.

   ____

8. Name a new invention.

   ____

9. Name an invention made of plastic.

   ____

10. Name an invention that goes in the water.

    ____

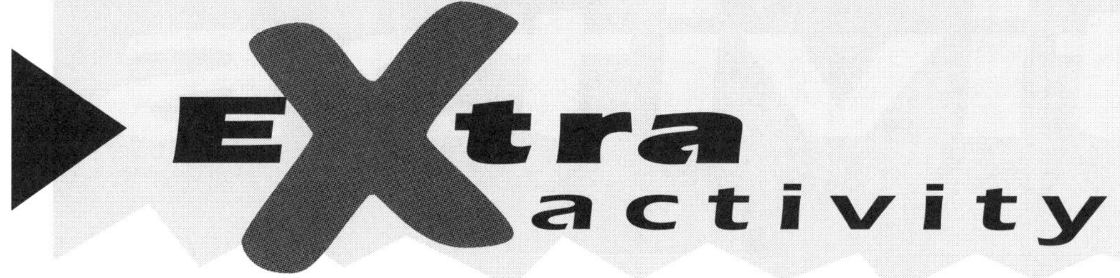

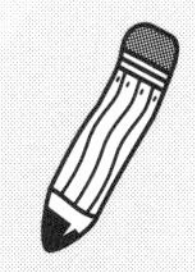

Guess the inventions.

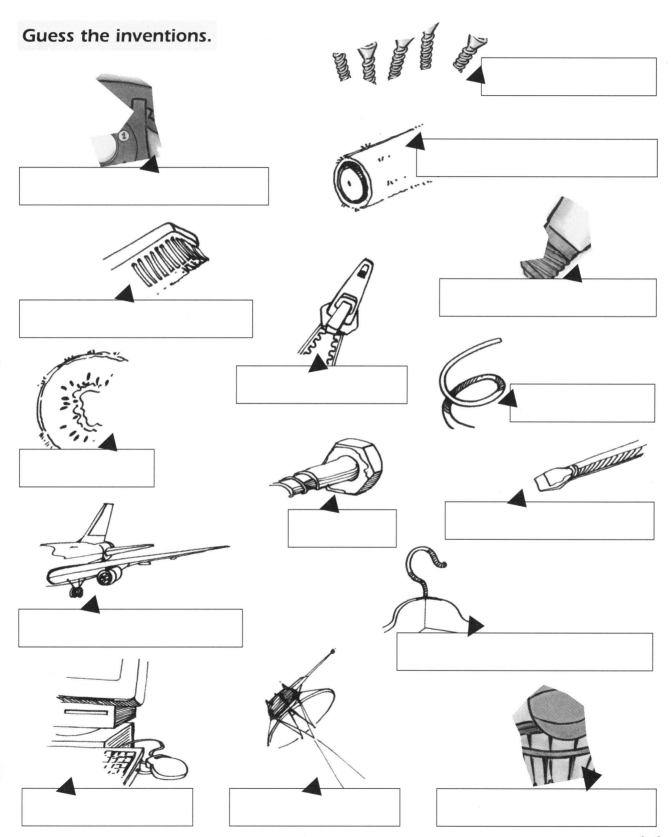

Check-up TIME

SB 91

This is what I learned.

	Yes ✔	No ✔
1 **I can name five inventions found in my home.**	❑	❑

2 **I know who invented these things.**

Yes ✔ ❑ No ✔ ❑

Yes ✔ ❑ No ✔ ❑

Yes ✔ ❑ No ✔ ❑

3 **I can name an old invention and its inventor.**

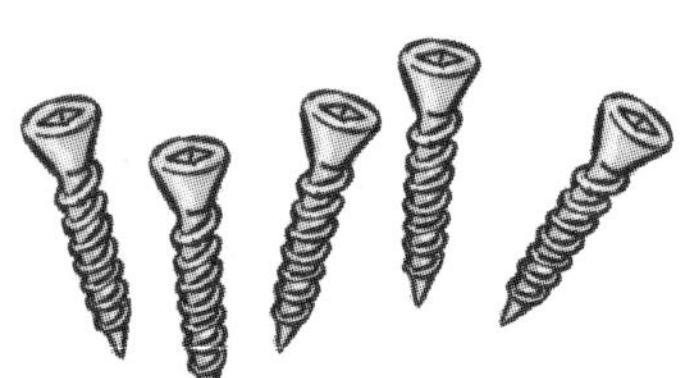

Yes ✔ ❑ No ✔ ❑

Yes ✔ ❑ No ✔ ❑

Yes ✔ ❑ No ✔ ❑

Reflection

	Yes ✔	No ✔
Did you . . .		
. . . take turns in your team?	❑	❑
. . . help your teammates?	❑	❑
Were you . . .		
. . . polite to your teammates?	❑	❑

UNIT 10

Snack Time

ACTIVITY 1

Food survey

Do you like . . .?	Like ✔	Don't like ✔
	❑	❑
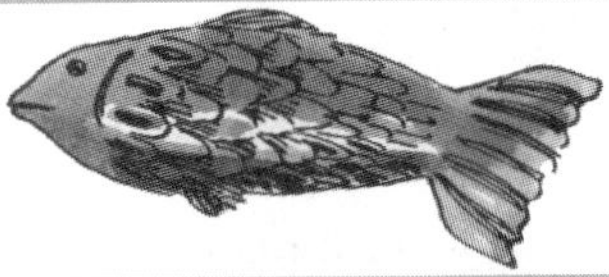	❑	❑
	❑	❑
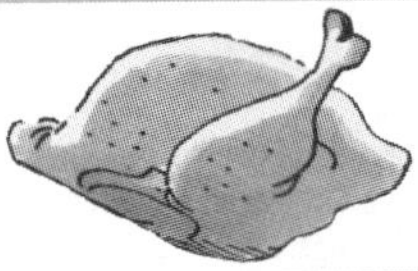	❑	❑
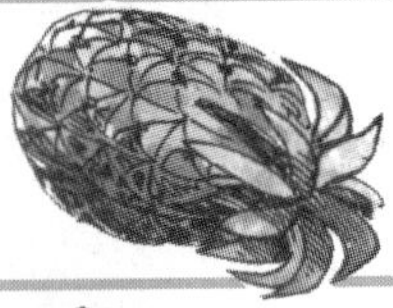	❑	❑
	❑	❑
	❑	❑
	❑	❑
	❑	❑
	❑	❑

Most popular food: ____________________

Least popular food: ____________________

ACTIVITY 2

What's in your lunch box?

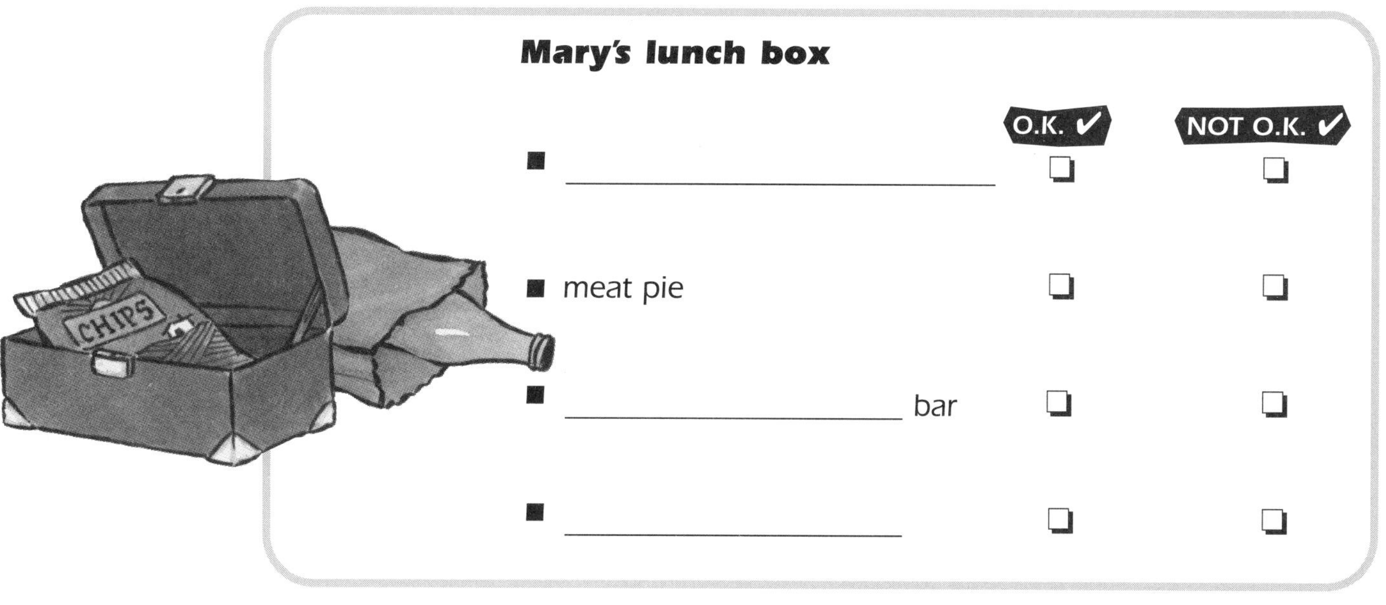

Mary's lunch box

	O.K. ✔	NOT O.K. ✔
■ ______________	❑	❑
■ meat pie	❑	❑
■ ____________ bar	❑	❑
■ ______________	❑	❑

Tom's lunch box

	O.K. ✔	NOT O.K. ✔
■ ______________	❑	❑
■ celery	❑	❑
■ ____________ sandwich	❑	❑
■ ______________	❑	❑

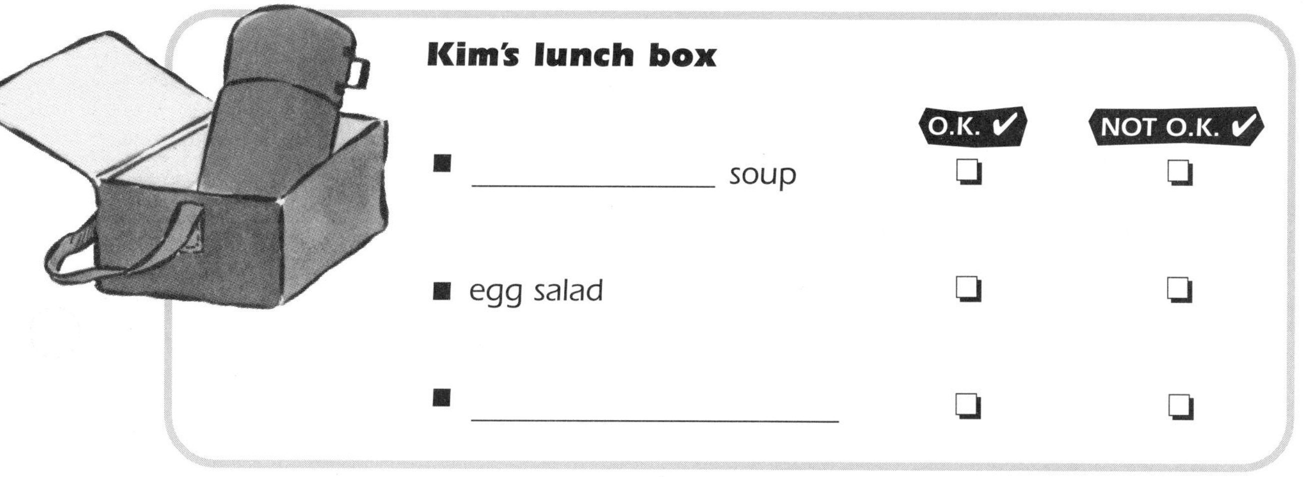

Kim's lunch box

	O.K. ✔	NOT O.K. ✔
■ ____________ soup	❑	❑
■ egg salad	❑	❑
■ ______________	❑	❑

ACTIVITY 3

Your favourite snack

My recipe

1 ______________________________

2 ______________________________

3 ______________________________

4 ______________________________

5 ______________________________

6 ______________________________

RECIPE: ____________________

INGREDIENTS: ____________________

INSTRUCTIONS:

1. ____________________
2. ____________________
3. ____________________
4. ____________________
5. ____________________
6. ____________________

Food groups: Put a check mark next to the food groups included in your recipe.

Fruits and vegetables ✔ ❑ Meat ✔ ❑

Bread and cereals ✔ ❑ Dairy products ✔ ❑

Extra activity

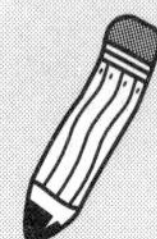

What am I?

1 I'm a fruit.

Monkeys love to eat me.

What am I? ______________________________

2 Children love to eat me in the summer.

I'm very cold.

I come in different flavours, like vanilla, chocolate, strawberry and even bubble gum.

What am I? ______________________________

3 Adults drink me at breakfast time.

I'm hot and brown.

What am I? ______________________________

4 I'm round and flat.

People pour syrup on me.

They eat me for breakfast.

What am I? ______________________________

Answers: banana, ice cream, coffee, pancake

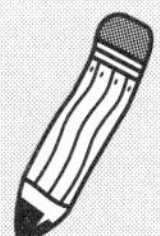

Now it's your turn. Describe two foods.
See if your classmates can guess what they are.

1 ______________________________

____

What am I?______________________________

2 ______________________________

____

What am I?______________________________

Check-up TIME

SB 100

This is what I learned.

I can . . .

	Yes ✓	No ✓	Unsure ✓
1. . . . talk about my favourite food.	❑	❑	❑
2. . . . name foods in their food groups.	❑	❑	❑
3. . . . write simple instructions for a recipe.	❑	❑	❑
4. . . . describe the foods in my lunch box.	❑	❑	❑
5. . . . say which foods make a healthy lunch.	❑	❑	❑

Reflection

Did you . . .

	Yes ✓	No ✓
. . . participate enthusiastically?	❑	❑
. . . contribute your ideas?	❑	❑

UNIT 11

Mischievous Sam

Story time: part one

Put the elements of the story in order.

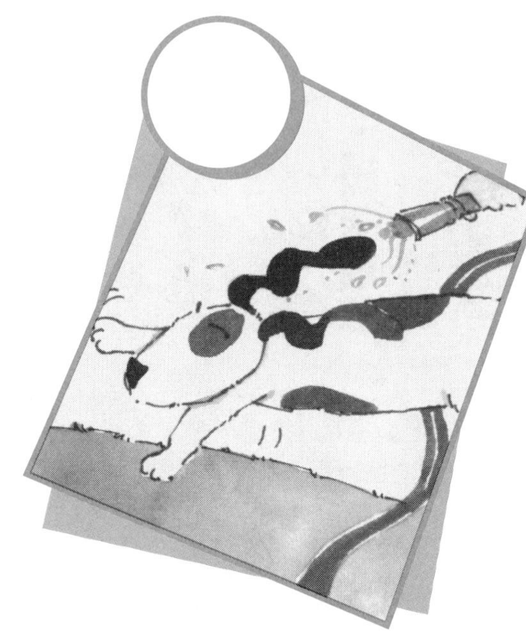

Story time: part two

Jokes	Difficult ✔	Messy ✔	O.K ✔	Dangerous ✔

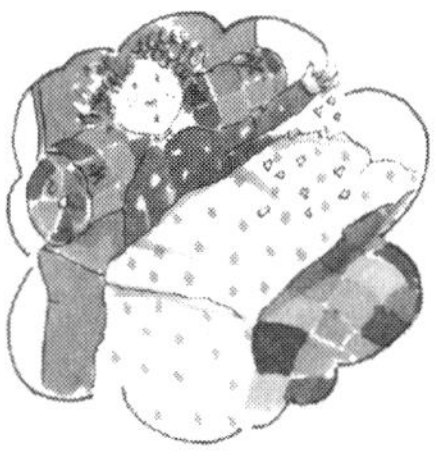				

What happens next?

My idea:

____

____

Watch out!

	Our jokes	Dangerous ✓	Difficult ✓	Messy ✓	O.K. ✓
1					
2					
3					
4					

Do not . . . ______________________________

____

____

____

ACTIVITY 5 Who is like me?

ACTIVITY 6 Making my own book

SB 111

My Ending

Draw the expressions.

That's cool!

Give me a break!

Get off it!

Piece of cake.

That's enough!

No kidding!

Check-up TIME

SB 112

This is what I learned.

1 **I can name all the characters.**

Yes ✓	No ✓	Unsure ✓
❑	❑	❑

2 **I can describe what happened.**

Yes ✓	❑	❑	❑	❑
No ✓	❑	❑	❑	❑
Unsure ✓	❑	❑	❑	❑

3 **I can understand the instructions.**

Yes ✓	❑	❑	❑	❑	❑
No ✓	❑	❑	❑	❑	❑
Unsure ✓	❑	❑	❑	❑	❑

Reflection

Did you . . .

	Yes ✓	No ✓	Unsure ✓
. . . help your partner?	❑	❑	❑
. . . encourage your partner?	❑	❑	❑
. . . take turns with your partner?	❑	❑	❑

UNIT 12

Sports Sensations

ACTIVITY 1

Sports for everyone

Match! Match!

1. Who can play baseball very well?
2. What can't Johnny do?
3. What can Philippe do?
4. What can't Josée do?

- kick a ball very far
- throw a ball into the basket
- Danielle
- roller skate

ACTIVITY 2

Something different

Guy

____

Sarah

____

Colin

____

ACTIVITY 3

What do you think?

SB 118

fun
dangerous
difficult
great
sensational
breathtaking
exciting

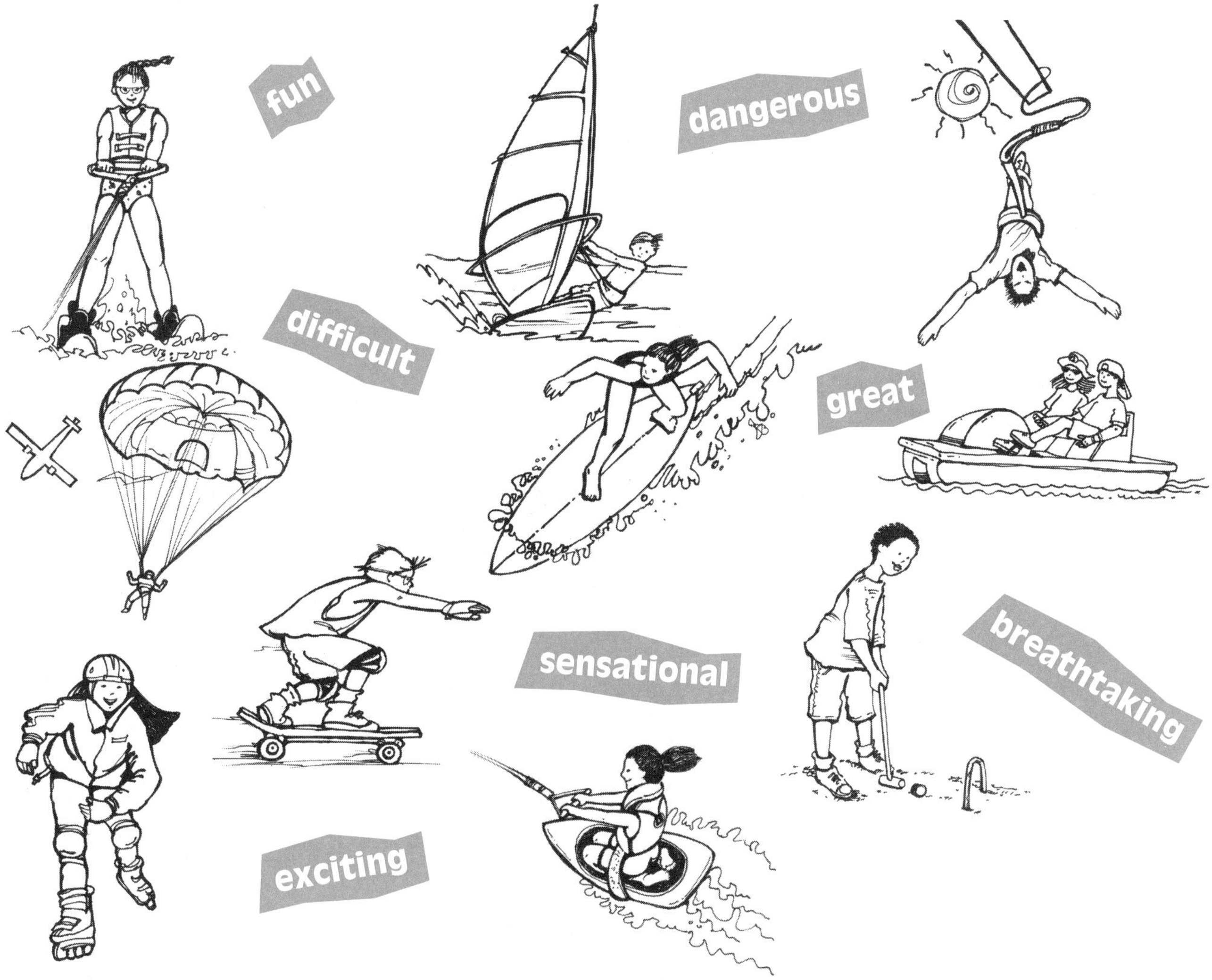

ACTIVITY 4

Nervous, sad, happy?

SB 119

Match! Match! Match!

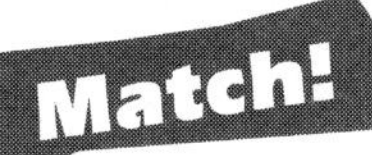

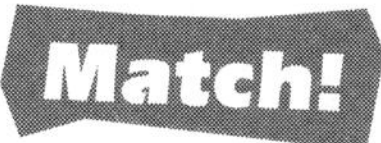

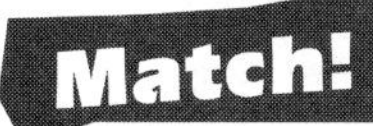

Sophie	I've got butterflies in my stomach.
Annie	I'm as happy as a lark.
Yves	I'm scared stiff.

Play the game!
Have fun!
SAY WHAT YOU THINK ABOUT HANG-GLIDING
MOVE FORWARD 3 SPACES.
DRAW
MIME
COMPLETE THE SENTENCE: I CAN . . .
COMPLETE THE SENTENCE: I CAN . . .
CAN YOU ROLLER SKATE?
SAY WHAT YOU THINK ABOUT BASEBALL.
MIME
DRAW
MOVE FORWARD 2 SPACES.
START HERE
MOVE BACK 1 SPACE.
MIME
SAY WHAT YOU THINK ABOUT SHOVEL RACING.
DRAW
FINISH LINE

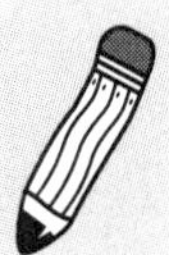

Find the mystery words!

- **Circle these words in the puzzle.**

badminton
baseball
breathtaking
cycling
exciting
field hockey
gymnastics
hang gliding
happy
kneeboarding
looks like
running
sad
scared
swimming
usual
walking

K	N	E	E	B	O	A	R	D	I	N	G
Y	B	A	D	M	I	N	T	O	N	N	N
E	E	X	C	I	T	I	N	G	I	H	I
K	R	U	N	N	I	N	G	D	A	V	K
C	L	O	O	K	S	L	I	K	E	I	A
O	A	N	C	Y	C	L	I	N	G	G	T
H	U	L	O	T	G	S	Y	P	P	A	H
D	S	O	F	G	N	I	K	L	A	W	T
L	U	F	N	S	C	A	R	E	D	U	A
E	B	A	S	E	B	A	L	L	N	D	E
I	H	S	W	I	M	M	I	N	G	A	R
F	G	Y	M	N	A	S	T	I	C	S	B

- **Look at the letters that remain. Find the mystery words.**

Mystery words: _ _ _ _ _ _   _ _ _ _   _ _   _ _ _

Mystery words: Having lots of fun

Check-up TIME

SB 122

This is what I learned.

	Yes ✓	No ✓
1 I can say which sports I can play.	❑	❑

2 I know these expressions.

I'm scared stiff.	I'm full of beans.	I've got butterflies in my stomach.	I'm as happy as a lark.
Yes ✓ ❑ No ✓ ❑	Yes ✓ ❑ No ✓ ❑	Yes ✓ ❑ No ✓ ❑	Yes ✓ ❑ No ✓ ❑

	Yes ✓	No ✓
3 I can describe the sports I play.	❑	❑

Reflection

Did you . . .

. . . talk quietly?	❑	❑
. . . take turns with your teammates?	❑	❑

UNIT 13

Bike Safety

ACTIVITY 1

What kind of cyclist are you?

SB 125

		True ✔	False ✔
1	I can't ride my bike with high heels.	❑	❑
2	I can easily ride my bike 1 km on the bicycle path.	❑	❑
3	I can be safer if I wear a helmet on my head.	❑	❑
4	I can be more energetic if I drink lots of water.	❑	❑
5	If I wear bright clothing, people can see me.	❑	❑

ACTIVITY 2

Accessories

SB 126

	Essential ✔	Not essential ✔	What students want ✔
pump	☐	☐	☐
gloves	☐	☐	☐
water bottle	☐	☐	☐
helmet	☐	☐	☐
bag	☐	☐	☐
red flag	☐	☐	☐
padlock	☐	☐	☐
horn	☐	☐	☐
mirrors	☐	☐	☐
sweater and bike shorts	☐	☐	☐

ACTIVITY 3

Traffic signs

SB 127

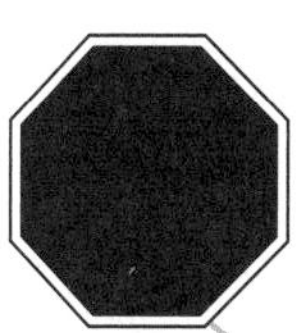

Turn right | Stop | Turn left | Slow down | Go | Cyclists only | Stop

ACTIVITY 4

Safety rules

SB 128

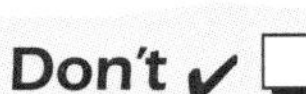
Do ✓ ❑ Don't ✓ ❑

Do ✓ ❑ Don't ✓ ❑

Do ✓ ❑ Don't ✓ ❑

Do ✓ ❑ Don't ✓ ❑

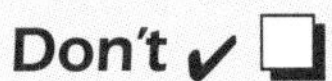
Do ✓ ❑ Don't ✓ ❑

Do ✓ ❑ Don't ✓ ❑

Do ✓ ❑ Don't ✓ ❑

My bicycle safety brochure

Title ______________________________

Bizarre biking!

Circle the 10 bizarre things.

Check-up TIME

SB 130

This is what I learned.

		Yes ✓	No ✓
1	**I can name the accessories I need.**	❑	❑
2	**I know what I must do when I see these signs.**	❑	❑

red

yellow

green

3	**I can understand Do rules and Don't rules.**	❑	❑

Reflection

Did you . . .

. . . encourage your partners?	❑	❑
. . . share ideas with your partners?	❑	❑
. . . listen well?	❑	❑

UNIT 14

The Case of the Missing Person

The case of the missing person, part one

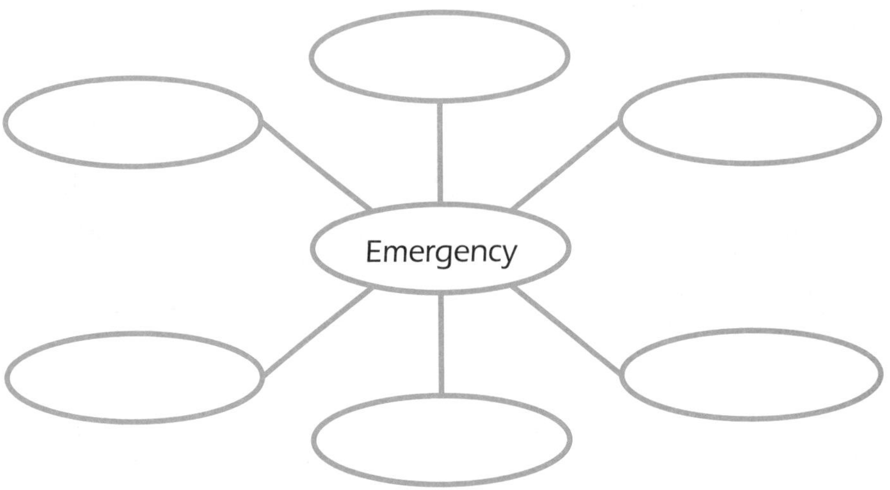

ACTIVITY 2

What's the problem?

SB 134

POLICE DEPARTMENT

Date: ______

Caller's family name: ______

Caller's first name: ______

Address: ______

______

______

Reason for the call: ______

The case of the missing person, part two

POLICE DEPARTMENT

POLICE REPORT: MISSING PERSON

First name: ______________________________

Family name: ______________________________

Age: ______________________________

Address: ______________________________

____

PHYSICAL DESCRIPTION

Hair: ____________________ Eyes: ____________________

Other physical characteristics: ______________________________

____

____

____

Other information: ______________________________

____

____

____

ACTIVITY 4

Is this really Ms Bernstein?

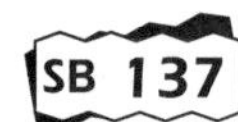

POLICE DEPARTMENT

POLICE ARTIST'S IMPRESSION

The case of the missing person, part three

How we think the story will end

____

____

____

What really happens

____

____

____

We were right ✔ ❑ wrong ✔ ❑

Your emergency guidelines

1 Whom to call or notify in an emergency

Police telephone number: ______________________

Friend's name
and telephone number: ______________________

____

Parent's or guardian's name
and work number: ______________________

____

Relative's name and
telephone number: ______________________

____

2 Information about yourself

Name: ______________________

Parent's or
guardian's name: ______________________

____

Address: ______________________

____

Colour of hair: ______________________

Colour of eyes: ______________________

Height: ______________________

Distinguishing features: ______________________

____

____

Have you seen this boy?

POLICE DEPARTMENT

POLICE REPORT: MISSING PERSON

Description

He is very tall. He has long red hair. His eyes are green. He has big, round blue glasses.

He's wearing a green and white T-shirt and blue jeans, running shoes and a baseball cap.

POLICE ARTIST'S IMPRESSION

Check-up TIME

SB 140

This is what I learned.

	Yes ✓	No ✓
1 **I can identify the main characters.**	❑	❑
2 **I can understand the description of a person.**	❑	❑
3 **I know whom to call in an emergency.**	❑	❑
4 **I know what to do in an emergency.**	❑	❑

Reflection

Did you . . .

. . . work well in your group?	❑	❑
. . . listen actively in your group?	❑	❑

UNIT 15

Far-out Facts

ACTIVITY 1

What do you know?

1

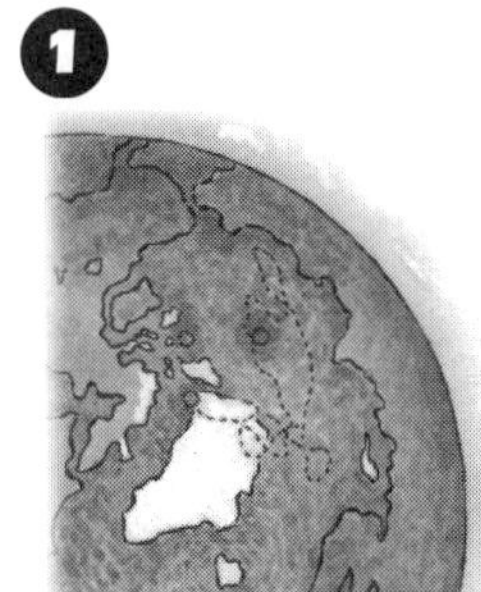

2

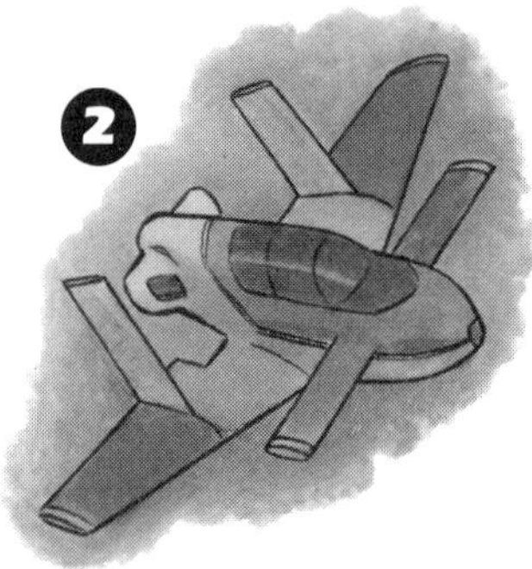

3

4

Fact #__________ Fact #__________ Fact #__________ Fact #__________

ACTIVITY 2

Amazing animal facts

1. ____________________ have tongues that are not dangerous.
2. ____________________ have dark tongues.
3. ____________________ cannot move their eyes.
4. ____________________ dance to warm up their hives.

ACTIVITY
3

Dinostory

SB 145

Where?
Who?

What happened?
What happens at the end?

ACTIVITY 4

Dinosaur world

ACTIVITY 5

What's that fact?

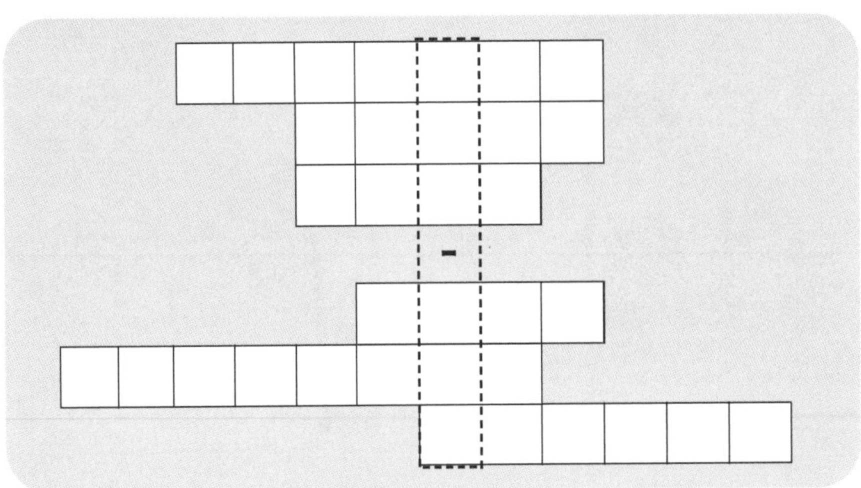

The hidden word is ____ ____ ____-____ ____ ____ .

It means ______________________________ .

Ready to play the Far-Out Fact Game?

Yes ✓
No ✓
We've made the die. ❏ ❏
We understand the rules. ❏ ❏
MISS YOUR TURN
1
2
We're ready!

CLOSURE

SB 151

Play the Far-Out Fact game!

Choose the right word.

big

large

small

long

taller

short

biggest

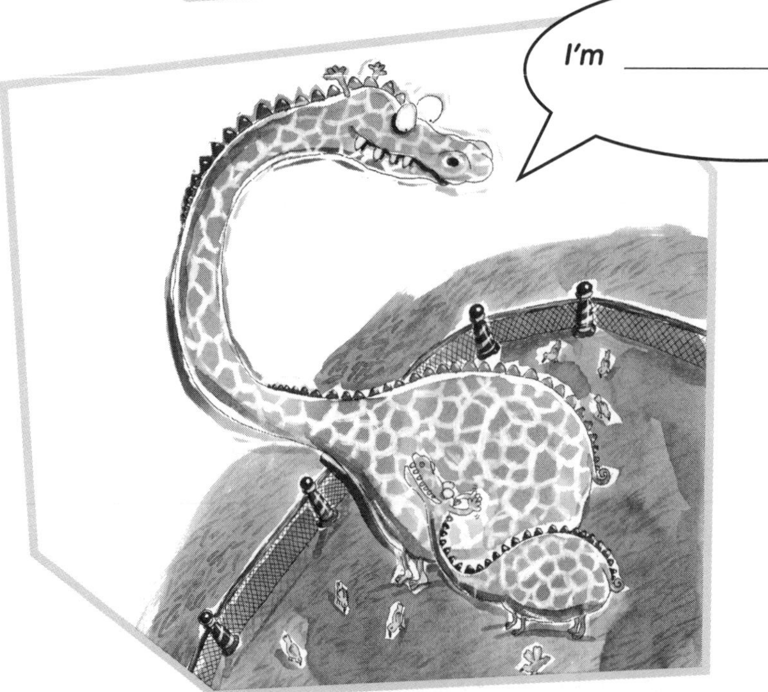

I have ______________________ eyes.

I am ____________________ .

I'm ____________________ .

Check-up TIME

SB 152

This is what I learned.

		Yes ✓	No ✓
1	I learned some new facts.	❑	❑
2	I can tell my partner two facts about dinosaurs.	❑	❑
3	I know what happened to dinosaurs.	❑	❑

Reflection

Did you . . .

	Yes ✓	No ✓
. . . encourage your classmates?	❑	❑
. . . help your teammates?	❑	❑

UNIT 16

Cirque du Soleil

ACTIVITY 1

Come one, come all!

Where?

When?

QUIDAM

Who?

ACTIVITY 2

Discover Cirque du Soleil

Places visited	Shows	Performers	Other information

ACTIVITY 3 Quidam

1. The name of the show is ______________________.

2. Cirque du Soleil presented *Quidam* in ______________________ and ______________________.

3. Cirque du Soleil presented *Quidam* for the first time on ______________________.

4. The performers are from ____________, ____________, ____________, ____________, ____________, ____________ and ____________.

5. Part of the music for the show is ______________________.

ACTIVITY 4 One great big family

Participant	Role
Mme Corporation	
Anne Lepage	
Les Flounes	
Guy Laliberté	
Franco Dragone	

Our circus collage

EXPANSION ACTIVITY

The circus game

Play the circus card game. Have fun!

Look at the letters on the juggler's pins.

Think of some words related to Cirque du Soleil that start with these letters.

C
circus

A
Alegria

S
show

F
family

B
blue

Check-up TIME

SB 161

This is what I learned.

	Yes ✓	No ✓
1 I can understand an invitation.	❑	❑
2 I can talk about Cirque du Soleil.	❑	❑

Reflection

Did you . . .

. . . talk when it was your turn?	❑	❑
. . . listen well?	❑	❑

UNIT 17

Let's Vacation

Hey, it's vacation time!

What are you going to do this summer?

What can you do in your neighbourhood?

	NAME	CITY	ACTIVITY	CAN ✓	CAN'T ✓
	____________	Drummondville	____________		
	Vincent	____________	____________		
	____________	Trois-Rivières	____________		
	____________	____________	reading		

ACTIVITY 3

How about a day camp?

Part one

Match! Match! Match!

1. Monday
2. Tuesday
3. Wednesday
4. Thursday
5. Friday

- arts and crafts
- swimming at the pool
- treasure hunt
- Olympic sports day
- backyard camping

Part two

NAME	Agree ✓	Disagree ✓
________________	❑	❑
________________	❑	❑
________________	❑	❑

ACTIVITY 4

Places to visit

A

Commercial # _______

B

Commercial # _______

C

Commercial # _______

D

Commercial # _______

ACTIVITY 5

It's my vacation.

I like to ______________________________ .

My teammates like to ______________________________

____

______________________________ .

Our vacation collage

Same or different?

Same or different?

1 

2 

3  

4  

5  

6  

7  

8  

9  

10  

11  

12

13  

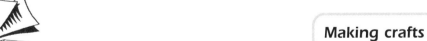

- Fishing
- Roller blading
- Playing baseball
- Going for a picnic
- Riding a bike
- Swimming
- Playing soccer
- Camping
- Reading
- Making crafts
- Playing tennis
- Going to the beach
- Playing badminton

Check-up TIME

SB 171

This is what I learned.

	Yes ✓	No ✓
1 I can suggest three activities to my friends.	❑	❑
2 I can ask my friends what they like.	❑	❑

3 I can name these activities.

Yes ✓ ❑ No ✓ ❑

Yes ✓ ❑ No ✓ ❑

Yes ✓ ❑ No ✓ ❑

Yes ✓ ❑ No ✓ ❑

Yes ✓ ❑ No ✓ ❑

Reflection

Did you . . .

. . . listen to your teammates?	❑	❑
. . . share your ideas and opinions?	❑	❑

Was . . .

. . . your team able to make decisions?	❑	❑

Songs

SONG 1

How are you?

Which expressions do you hear in the song?

	Yes ✓	No ✓
Hello.	❑	❑
How are you?	❑	❑
I'm so pleased to meet you.	❑	❑
Goodbye.	❑	❑
So long.	❑	❑
See you soon.	❑	❑
Good morning.	❑	❑
Good afternoon.	❑	❑

When you meet someone, you say

____

______________________________.

When you leave someone, you say

____

________________________.

SONG 2

Months and days

CALENDAR

SUNDAY						

My favourite month

numbers

Colours

STUDENT A

Name that colour!

1. Grass ____________________

2. Banana ____________________

3. Sky ____________________

4. Quarter ____________________

5. Snow ____________________

6. Night ____________________

7. A fruit ____________________

8. Valentine's Day ____________________

9. Shoes ____________________

10. A flower ____________________

STUDENT B

Name that colour!

1. St Patrick's cloverleaf ____________________

2. Sun ____________________

3. Ocean water ____________________

4. A metal ____________________

5. Clouds ____________________

6. No light ____________________

7. Yellow and red ____________________

8. Apple ____________________

9. Autumn ____________________

SONG 5 Family love

SONG 6 Magic

Check the tricks mentioned in the song.

SONG 7
Doing the Body Twist

SONG 8
Going on vacation

Find someone who . . . on vacation.

		NAME	NAME
1	. . . goes horseback riding	__________	__________
2	. . . goes fishing	__________	__________
3	. . . plays baseball	__________	__________
4	. . . plays soccer	__________	__________
5	. . . plays hockey	__________	__________
6	. . . goes on a trip	__________	__________
7	. . . goes to the ocean	__________	__________
8	. . . visits family and friends	__________	__________
9	. . . goes to summer camp	__________	__________
10	. . . goes camping	__________	__________

Songs

SONG 1

How are you today?

Hello, how are you today?
Everybody say
"Hello, how are you today?"
I'm so pleased to meet you.
I'm happy to be with you.
Hello, how are you today?

Goodbye, so long, see you soon.
Bye-bye, so long, see you soon.
Must go now, see you later.
Got to leave now, alligator.
Goodbye, so long, see you soon.

Good morning, boys and girls,
How are you?
Good afternoon, boys and girls,
How are you?
It's great to be here,
So nice to be near.
Hello, boys and girls,
How are you?

SONG 2

Months and days

January, February, March, April and May,
June, July, August, September
All have beautiful days.
October, November and December
Are nice in their way.
Now that we know the months of the year,
Let's all learn the days.

Monday, Tuesday, Wednesday, Thursday, Friday
Are all weekdays.
Saturday, Sunday, Saturday, Sunday
Are my favourite days.
Monday, Tuesday, Wednesday, Thursday and Friday
Are all school days.
Now that we know the days of the week,
Hey, guys, what do we say? We say,

O.K. ALL TOGETHER NOW:

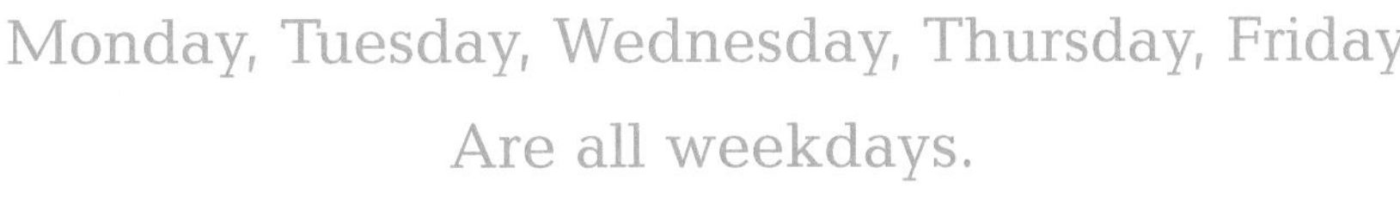

Monday, Tuesday, Wednesday, Thursday, Friday
Are all weekdays.
Saturday, Sunday, Saturday, Sunday
Are my favourite days.
Monday, Tuesday, Wednesday, Thursday, Friday,
Saturday and Sunday.
Now that we know the days and the months,
Let's go out and play.

SONG 3

Numbers

One plus one is two.
This is what we can do.
Two plus one is three,
Come and dance with me.
Three plus one is four,
Everyone stand on the floor.
Four plus one is five,
Wave your hands, people arrive.

I know my numbers:
1, 2, 3, 4, 5.
I know my numbers:
Have fun counting to five.

Six plus one is seven,
Flap your arms like a chicken.
Seven plus one is eight,
Make a smile: you look great.
Eight plus one is nine,
Don't stop, you look so fine.
Nine plus one is ten,
Let's all sing it again.

I know my numbers:
6, 7, 8, 9, 10.
I know my numbers:
I can count up to ten.

Colours

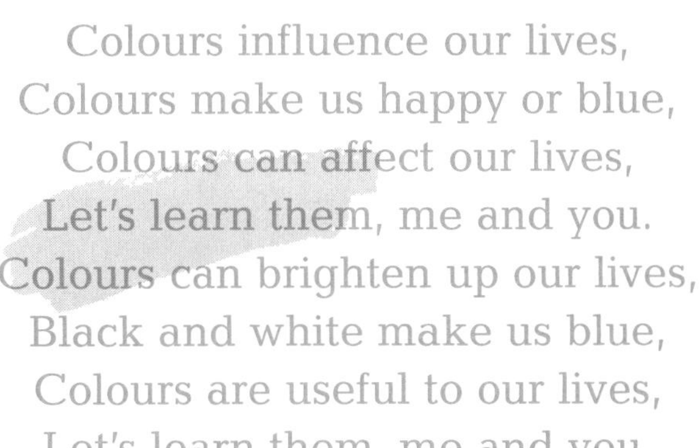

Colours influence our lives,
Colours make us happy or blue,
Colours can affect our lives,
Let's learn them, me and you.
Colours can brighten up our lives,
Black and white make us blue,
Colours are useful to our lives,
Let's learn them, me and you.

We've got green for the grass that grows all summer,
Yellow for the leaves in the fall,
White for the snow that stays all winter,
Hey! And that's not all.
We've got grey for the spring when the snow melts,
Blue for the sky up above,
Red for a setting sunset,
Now we can sing all about . . .

Colours! Green, yellow and white.
Colours! Grey, blue and red.
Colours are coming my way.
Colours! Black, orange and gold.
Colours! Silver, brown, violet.
Colours! Let's learn them today.

We've got black for the night when it's dark out,
Orange is the fruit that we eat,
Gold is for a precious metal,
Hey! What do you think?
Silver for a quarter we buy with,
Brown for the earth that we dig,
Violet is a beautiful flower,
Now we can sing all about . . .

SONG 5

Family love

If you have love within your family,
Love you are willing to share,
Respect within the family
Will come if you really care.
Patience with the people in your family.
Treat them with love and care,
And the love that you find
Will last to the end of time,
For when you love, love will be there.

SONG 6

Magic

Do you believe in a magic tree?
Do you believe in what you see?
Birds that appear from nowhere,
People who come from nowhere.

Do you believe in magic?
Do you believe in what you see?
Do you believe in magic?
Will you believe it when you see
Tricks done for you and me?
Magic . . . Magic . . .

Do you believe in magic cards,
Tricks that are easy, tricks that are hard?
Do you believe in a magic act,
Pulling out rabbits from a hat?

Do you believe in a magic show?
Do you see? Do you know?
Do you believe in magic sticks?
Do you like to play some tricks?

SONG 7

Doing the Body Twist

Put your hands in the air and make them do the Twist.
Move your fingers in the air and make them do the Twist.
Swing your arms in the air and do the Body Twist.

Put your finger on your nose and turn it round and round.
Put your hand on your mouth and blow everyone a kiss.
Blink your eyes at a person and do the Body Twist.

We're doing the Body Twist!
We're doing the Body Twist!
Shake your shoulders in a Body Twist,
Move your legs in a Body Twist,
Close your eyes, rub your ears,
Jump to your feet, point your toes.
Everybody's doing the Body Twist!

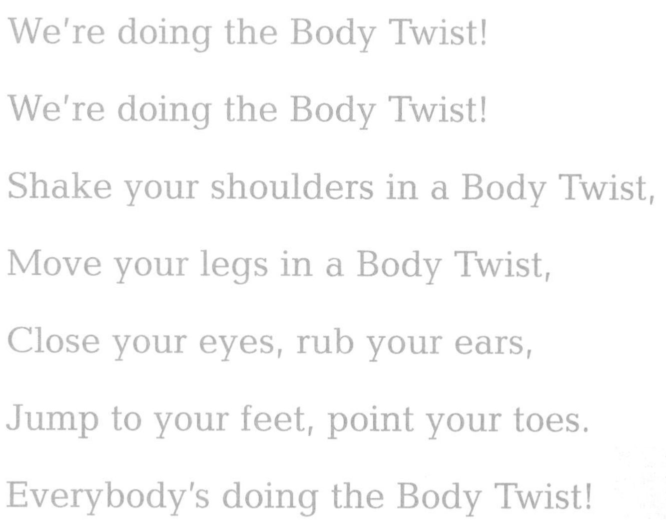

Bend your knees, draw a circle
And move them round and round.
Now move your hips in a circle
And move them round and round.
Twist your body in a circle
And do the Body Twist!

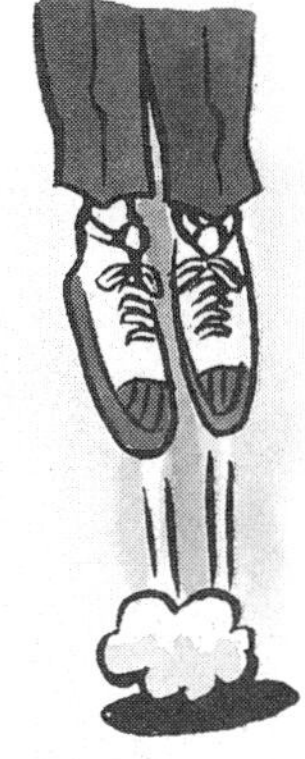

SONG 8

Going on vacation

What are you doing on vacation,
Doing on vacation?
I am gonna have fun.
Are you going on vacation,
Going on vacation?
Yes and I'm gonna have fun.

I'm going horseback riding with Mom and Dad,
Going on a fishing trip won't be sad,
I'll play some baseball, soccer and some hockey too
And yes I'm gonna have fun.

I'm going with my mother to P.E.I.
Playing in the ocean, my oh my!
I'll see my cousins, aunts and uncles, hi hi hi!
And yes I'm gonna have fun.

What are we doing on vacation,
Doing on vacation?
We are gonna have fun.
Are we going on vacation,
Going on vacation?
Yes and we're gonna have fun.

We'll stay at home, watch TV every day,
Don't have no projects anyway.
We'll spend the rest of the summer in our own way
And yes we're gonna have fun.

1. Classroom talk

Colour in the pictures.

2. Colours

black | light blue | blue | dark blue | brown

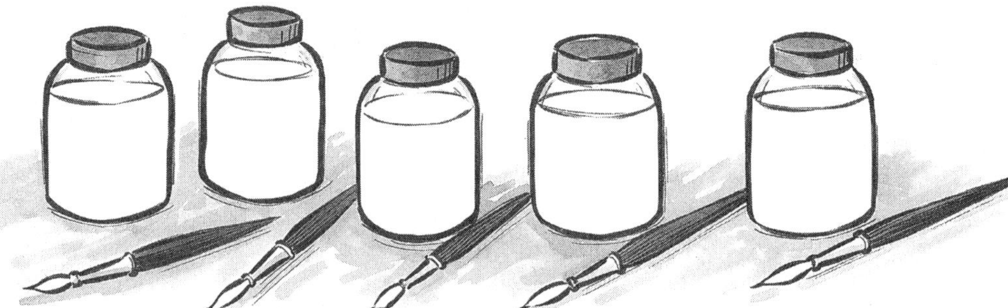

light green | green | dark green | grey | orange

pink | purple | red | yellow | white

hazel eyes | black hair | blond hair | red hair

3. Days of the week

There are seven days in a week.
There are four weeks in a month.
There are twelve months in a year.

Did you know?
In English, the names of the days of the week always start with a capital letter. For example, *Today is Monday.*

4. Months of the year

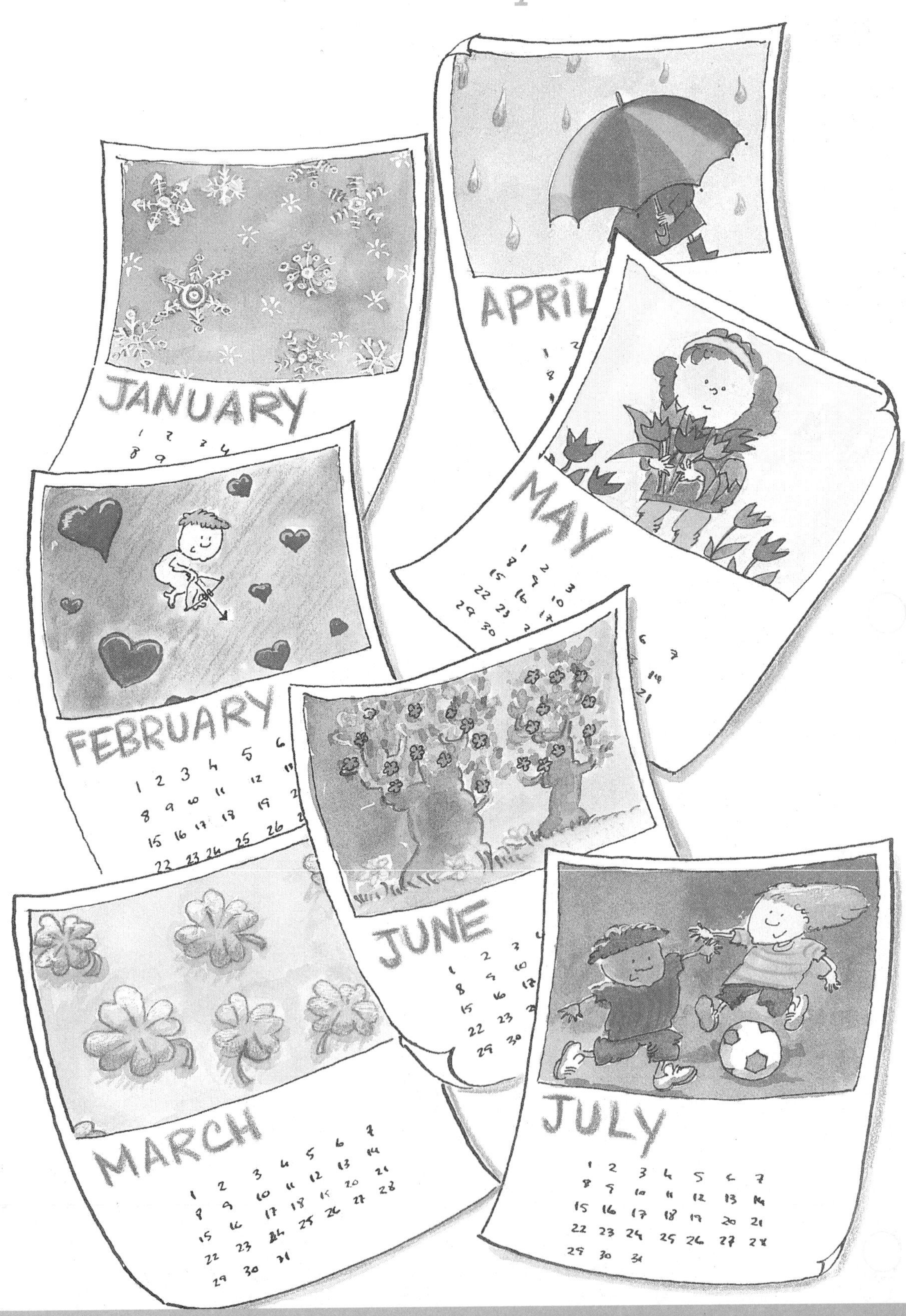

Did you know?
In English, the names of months start with a capital letter. The names of the seasons start with a lower-case letter. For example, *I love summer. My favourite month is July.*

The four seasons

March, April, May = spring
June, July, August = summer
September, October, November = fall
December, January, February = winter

5. Time

3 o'clock

3:15 OR a quarter past three

3:30 OR half past three

3:45 OR a quarter to four

midnight

noon

morning = a.m.

afternoon = p.m.

evening, night = p.m.

What time is it?
It's half past 10.

6. Numbers

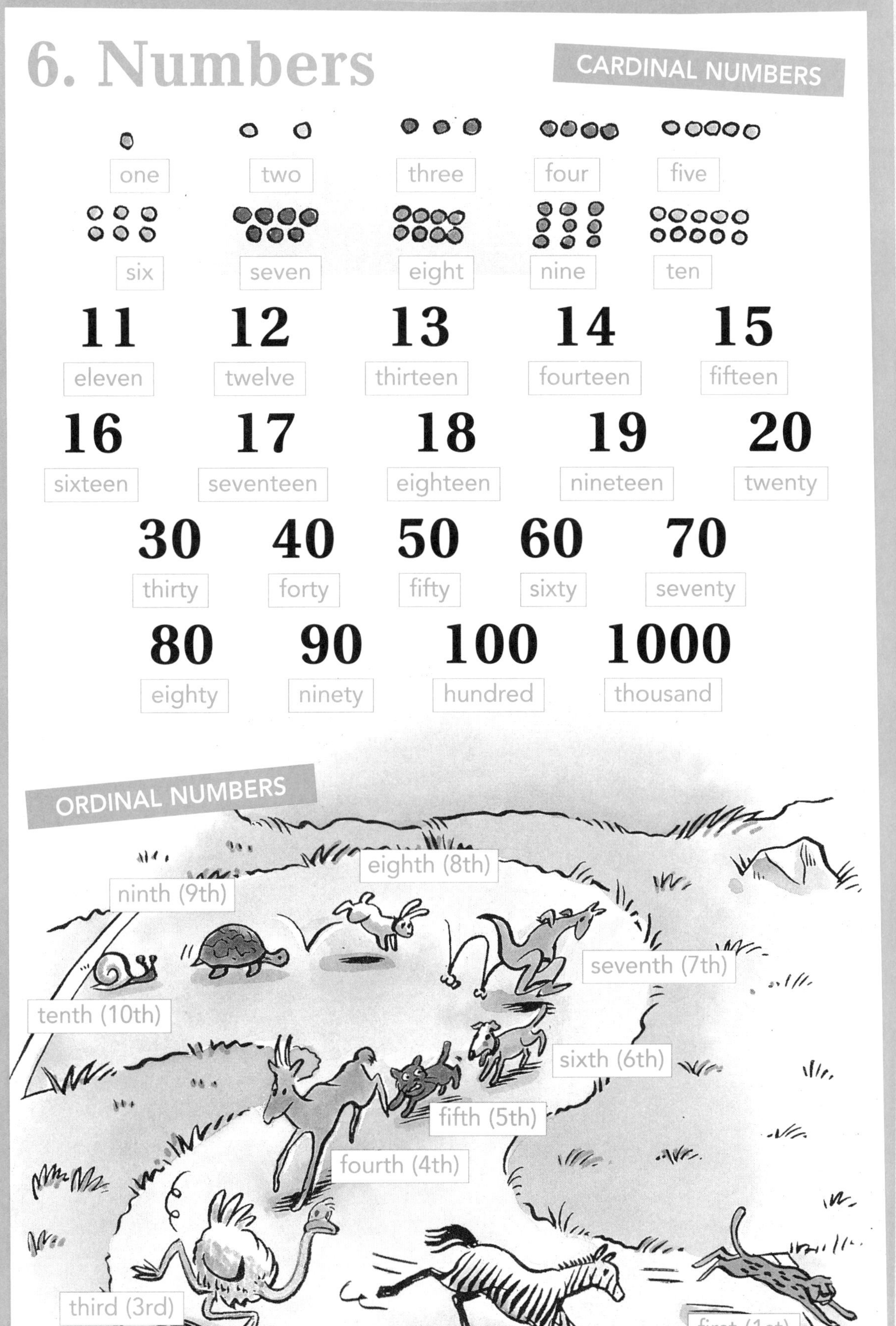

CARDINAL NUMBERS
one
two
three
four
five
six
seven
eight
nine
ten
11
eleven
12
twelve
13
thirteen
14
fourteen
15
fifteen
16
sixteen
17
seventeen
18
eighteen
19
nineteen
20
twenty
30
thirty
40
forty
50
fifty
60
sixty
70
seventy
80
eighty
90
ninety
100
hundred
1000
thousand
ORDINAL NUMBERS
eighth (8th)
ninth (9th)
seventh (7th)
tenth (10th)
sixth (6th)
fifth (5th)
fourth (4th)
third (3rd)
second (2nd)
first (1st)

7. Parts of the body

8. Food

corn
lettuce
carrots
onion
celery
cucumber
tomato
potatoes
mushrooms
broccoli
fish
eggs
milk
cheese
butter
grapefruit
kiwis
peach
bananas
ice cream
orange
apple
cream
yogurt
grapes
pear
bread
pineapple
doughnut
strawberries
cake
muffin
ham
turkey
soft drink
chicken
juice
coffee
tea
pasta
pork chop
steak

9. Some useful expressions

Ways to greet people
Good morning.
Hi!
Good afternoon.
Hello.
Hi there.
Good evening.
Ways to say goodbye
Bye-bye.
So long.
Goodbye.
See you later.
See you.
Ways to say "That's dangerous"
Be careful.
Watch out!
Look out!
Ways to congratulate someone
Fantastic!
Good job!
Super!
Great!
Well done.

Ways to thank someone

Thank you.

Thanks a lot.
Thank you very much.

Ways to ask for help

Please can you help me?

Please give me a hand.

Ways to ask for clarification

Please say that again.
Can you repeat that, please?
What does that mean?
How do you say that in English?
I don't understand. Please can you explain?

Ways to apologize

Pardon me.

Sorry about that.
Excuse me.
I beg your pardon.

I'm very sorry.

10. Some useful question words

Questions about a thing (= What?)

Questions about a person (= Who?)

Who's that?
That's my friend Brian.
Who's your teacher?
Mr Samson.
Who is she?
She's Brian's sister, Mary.
Who are they?
They're the twins, Philippe and Olivier.
Who's your best friend?
Jonathan. See, there he is.

Questions about a place (= Where?)

Where do you come from?
Where do you live?
Where are you going this weekend?

In Montréal.
Chicoutimi.
To visit my grand-parents in Québec.

Questions about time (= When? What time?)

When is your birthday?

October 23.

When is your English class?
What time are you leaving?
SCHOOL AGENDA

On Wednesday.
At 4 o'clock.

Questions about feelings and age (= How?)

Hi, Bob. How are you?

I'm fine, thanks.

How old are you today, Marie?

I'm 9.
How do you feel?

Great!

Questions about quantity (= How many? OR How much?)

How many brothers and sisters do you have?
I have one half-sister and no brothers.

How much cake would you like?
Just a small piece, please.
Mom, I need a new bicycle helmet.
How much does it cost?
$19.95.

Questions about ability or permission (= Can?)

Can I go swimming with my friend, please?

Yes you can.

Can you swim under water?

Sure I can.